Why Magical Rites? Why look to the Crystal Well?

In Nature, and in the Earth, we look and find Beauty. Within ourselves we find a Well from which we may draw Truth and Knowledge. And when we draw from this Well, we re-discover that we are all Children of the Earth.

Relating to the Earth, and to Nature's rhythms and cycles, we nourish our roots and find Magic.

These simple rites are presented to you as a means of finding your own way back to Nature; for discovering and experiencing the Beauty and the Magic of unity with the Source.

These are Celebrations of the Seasons; at the same time they are rites by which we attune ourselves to the flow of the Force — the Energy of Life. These are Rites of Passage by which we celebrate the major transitions we all experience in life; by which each life joins with All-life.

These are Rites of Magick by which we celebrate the special place of humanity as an agent of Creative Love between 'Heaven and Earth'; and by which we, ourselves, grow to fulfill our Spiritual Potential.

And here, too, you will find the Craft for Living Life Well. In this book of beauty and wisdom, you have — if you wish it — a guide to a way of life that offers more by opening channels to the Greater World—visible and invisible — that is both around and within you.

This way of life will not conflict with any offered you by church or temple, but it will, at the same time, restore to you the sense of rootedness with the Earth — even if you live and work in the concrete jungle of the urban-industrial complex.

Here are the Old Ways, but they are also Ways for Today.

In our hearts, we are all Pagans — for we are all *pagani*, people of the country, born of Earth. There is wisdom in knowing your origins, and from your roots you may draw strength and knowledge. Some call this way *Wise-Craft*, or *Wicca*. Call it what you will, or call it nothing at all . . . but *listen! Your Mother, the Earth, is calling to you, Her child.*

In this book are the ways to listen and to love, to give and to receive, to learn and to live, to adore and to find the way to the Divine Source within.

—*Carl Llewellyn Weschcke*

About the Author

ED FITCH is one of the leaders in today's neo-Paganism and Wicca. A longtime High Priest of Gardnerian Witchcraft, he is one of the group of Craft scholars who set up the Pagan Way during the late 1960s. He personally researched and wrote the basic cycle of rituals for that system . . . rites acclaimed for their poetry and depth, as well as their beauty.

Ed is particularly a researcher into folklore, mythology, and ancient literature, with a special interest in North and Central Europe, the Slavonic lands, and Britain. He has had a notable interest in the reconstruction of rituals and legends from the fragments and shards which have come down to us in ancient literature and from recent archeological findings. For several years he published the neo-Romantic Journal of modern Paganism, *The Crystal Well*, a magazine unique in its visual and literary excellence, and the source of most of the material in this book.

He has travelled widely throughout his life, in this country and abroad. A former Air Force officer with many years of service, he is now an aerospace engineer residing in Southern California.

To Write to the Author

We cannot guarantee that every letter written to the author can be answered, but all will be forwarded on to him. Both the author and the publisher appreciate hearing from readers, learning of your enjoyment and benefit from this book. The authors sometimes participate in seminars and workshops, and dates and places are announced in the *Llewellyn New Times* newspaper. To write to the author, or to ask a question, or to secure a free copy of this newspaper, write to:

Ed Fitch
c/o LLEWELLYN PUBLICATIONS
P.O. Box 64383-MR, St. Paul, MN 55164-0383, U.S.A.

Please enclose a self-addressed, stamped envelope for reply, or $1.00.

Magical Rites from the Crystal Well

by
Ed Fitch
and
Janine Renee

Original Art by
John Goodier

1984
Llewellyn Publications
St. Paul, MN 55164-0383, U.S.A.

International Standard Book Number: 0-87542-230-6
Library of Congress Number: 83-80134
First Edition: 1984

Library of Congress Cataloging in Publication Data

Fitch, Ed.
    Magical rites from the crystal well.

    (Llewellyn's practical magick series)
    Bibliography: p.
    1. Magic.   2. Rites and Ceremonies.   I. Title.
II. Series.
BF1611.F53   1984   133.4'3   83-80134
ISBN 0-87542-230-6

Cover and Original Art: John Goodier
Book Design: Terry Buske
Produced by Llewellyn Publications
Typography and Art property of Chester-Kent, Inc.

Published by
LLEWELLYN PUBLICATIONS
A Division of Chester-Kent, Inc.
P.O. Box 64383
St. Paul, MN 55164-0383, U.S.A.
Printed in the United States of America

Contents

rystal Well magazine was around for a fairly long time . . . since 1965, to be exact. Starting off as an occasionally published mimeographed newsletter, it eventually grew to be a scholarly, good-sized magazine which often managed to come out quarterly. Quite a variety of subjects were covered, but the most popular always seem to have been the rituals.

The rituals have been quite varied: seasonal, magical, specialized, general . . . whatever the directions of our current researches happened to be at the time. These studies have always been of major importance to those of us who worked on the magazine and in the Craft. There is a very great amount of Pagan lore which can be drawn from history, literature, anthropological researches, and many other areas . . . if one knows where to search, and is willing to do a lot of work in digging it out.

Over the years numerous readers, as well as many of the staff, have suggested publishing one or more compilations of these rites, though time and money always seemed to be in short supply. But we knew that sooner or later this sort of thing had to be attempted; in our rapidly changing modern world the publishing of one's researches gives at least some chance of keeping them available to the public. Magazines and newsletters seem to vanish like summer dew.

And we want the Old Ways of Paganism and of the Wicca to be around for a long time; we want to have something that is pleasing to the psyche and provocative to the imagination to be on the bookshelves in decades to come. In time a new generation will arrive which will be looking for something of quality and depth. Hopefully this can be part of our legacy.

The rituals and background lore herein represent a full cycle of material . . . perhaps enough to base a full tradition on, and definitely enough to enrich and expand existing books maintained by Witches and Pagans. We can't claim that it's a fully self-consistent system based on totally fundamental folk roots and the most ancient Mysteries: that sort of lore is still being researched.

What you hold in your hand is a carefully researched and restored volume of material based primarily on Central and Eastern European lore, as well as that of the British Isles. It's all been around, in quite similar form, for centuries or possibly millenia.

The past can have a lot to offer us, and can point the way to an even better and more challenging future.

Preface

The world can be molded and improved in many ways, and humankind itself has the potential for veritable godhood. By gaining a deep realization of our most ancient foundations, and by constantly re-establishing our essential oneness with all of nature, we can make both ourselves and the universe at large into works of ever greater perfection.

This volume, and the material within it, provide for a few steps towards that high goal. The inner drive and the questing, adventurous spirit, are something that *you* must provide.

Best of fortune be with you, friends. And may the blessings of the Lady ever be yours.

Blessed Be,
Ed Fitch
April 1982, C.E.

his book has been compiled to provide modern pagans with rituals and with suggestions for festival practices which will help us return to our ancient roots. Paganism is a joyous yet reverent philosophy which everyone can share in — for there is not a person alive in the world today who is not descended from Pagan ancestors.

We like to describe ourselves as "Neopagans" because we've taken the most worthwhile philosophies and practices of the Pagan religions of ancient times, and adapted them to modern needs and life-styles.

According to our definition, a Neopagan is a person who believes that the Divinity or "God-force" is contained within all living beings and in the material world as well, (this belief is known as "Monism"—God is "one" with the Universe); and who follows a religion which honors and observes the cycles of nature.

Although our Pagan ancestors honored — even deified — natural forces in their religions, they did so because their lives were dependent upon these forces for successful hunting and a good harvest. Today, life is very much changed, and the average person is practically divorced from nature, and it would not be feasible for most of our modern Pagans to try to return to the more natural life-styles of the past. Therefore, modern Paganism concentrates on a more spiritual ideal . . . striving for higher consciousness and spirituality . . . but we do continue to revere the Earth-Mother, the power and beauty of the natural Universe, and the universal Archetypes within ourselves. By living in harmony with the rhythms, the tides, and the forces of the Cosmos, we will be more complete persons . . . enjoying health of body, strength of mind, and greatness of soul.

The set of rites and practices contained herein comprises our own system, which we've developed for use by our students and our friends. I'm afraid we've not yet devised a name for our particular brand or denomination of Neopaganisms.

Our rituals are deeply reverent and rich in symbolic content, but they are best performed where there is privacy. It is very sad that religious bigotry can still flourish in a nation that was founded on freedom of belief. Even though morals, ethics, and clean living are important to our way of life, we find it necessary to practice our religion in a subdued manner. We do not want to draw attention to ourselves and abuse to our children from people who may be prejudiced

Introduction

against a religion which is different from their own. Usually this prejudice is based solely upon misinformation and ignorance.

There are also a number of falsehoods circulating about Neopagan religious practices . . . . drug abuse, promiscuity, animal sacrifice, and worse . . . and although we may try our best to be above board in every way, it may be a long time yet before we can put down these nasty accusations . . . accusations which were originally contrived so that the Church could have a justification for executing all of its rivals. Today no one believes that Jews murder and eat little babies as part of their religious rituals — yet that belief was common in the Middle Ages. The Jewish faith has now won respectability, and by being exemplary in our moral behaviour and social usefulness, we also hope eventually to attain acceptance and respectability.

One of the beauties of Paganism is its adaptability.

A nature religion must necessarily be attuned to climate, geography, and locale. And any religion, to be effective, must be attuned to the needs of the individual. Therefore, we do not expect our readers to take this little book of rites as a "bible," — the rituals herein are rather generalized, — deliberately so, because that lends them flexibility. We expect the reader to use these rites merely as a guideline, embellishing upon them or altering them to suit the needs of self, family, and grove.* Calendrical dates may particularly require adjustment — the arrival of Spring, the Harvest ingathering, and the onset of Winter are all dates that vary widely from area to area. We tend to use the traditional dates for these festivals for the purposes of this book because they are good arbitrary dates.

You will also notice that we usually do not use any Goddess or God names, we direct our invocations to certain personifications of nature. For example: " . . . Our Lady of the Harvest, The Mother Earth . . . " or " . . . Our Harvest Lord . . . The resplendent Sun King . . . " Naturally, if you are already accustomed to invoking certain ethnic or traditional god-names for these personifications, you may want to insert them into the rites, and you may also wish to insert invocations to any other deities that are of special importance to your household.

The festival calendar and meanings are generally patterned after the basic Neopagan systems that are

* A "grove" is a Pagan congregation.

wide-spread in this country now, and which we have been active in for many years.

The popular Neopagan systems are derived from European folk-traditions, but we have tried to modify and generalize them so that they'll have a more universal appeal. We have also made a study of nature-festivals from all over the world . . . India, Africa, North America, and so on, as well as the traditional Jewish holidays (which themselves derive from ancient nature religions), and practices taken from the Catholic Church which appear to have been taken from ancient pagan practices themselves. We have tried to incorporate elements of these other festivals wherever they will be meaningful and practical.

THE SIGN OF THE PENTAGRAM

The sign of the pentagram is often used during modern Pagan rites as a sign of salutation to the Great Ones and to the quarters. As far back as ancient Greece, and probably even in the Minoan Sea-Empire, the five-pointed star was the sign of the Goddess in her sea-aspect, often called "Astarte". It was a sign of protection, and (for example) sailors would have it tattooed on the thumb-mound of their palms for luck . . . something which you still occasionally see today.

But the pentagram as we have it now is a borrowing from Ceremonial Magick, especially the Golden Dawn system practices, which have become standard. As such, it is relatively modern . . . perhaps Medieval in this particular form.

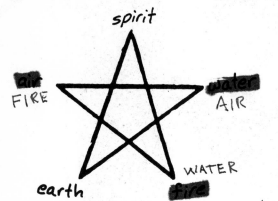

The pentagram represents the concept of "man made perfect" . . . incorporating the concepts of the elemental universe within the body and soul of man, the macrocosm within the microcosm. The points on the pentagram are usually assigned as in the diagram at left.

There is a complex system of invoking and banishing for each of the elements, which is of ceremonialist origin and which is used by some Wicca groups. Most, however, use a simplified version, as in the diagram below:

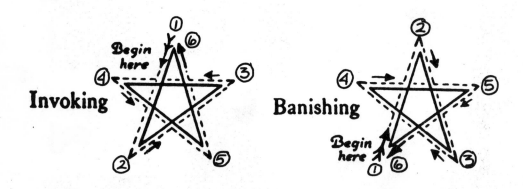

Usually the pentagram is drawn in the air with the athame, visualizing it in the mind as scribing a glowing blue star in the air, to be sent forth with the final salute after kissing the blade. In many groups the priestess draws the pentagram while other members just raise their own athames in a simple salute; in others they all do it together. The pentagram may also be described with the sword, wand, or fingers in substitution for the athame.

It is necessary to mention here that for Pagan purposes, the pentagram need not even be drawn . . . this is an individual's or a group's matter of choice: a simple gesture of salutation (such as throwing a kiss) is all that is necessary. The concept of calling upon the four quarters is the archaic method.

The banishing pentagram is also effective as a simple form of protection when drawn in the air to banish any negative influences which the individual may regard as threatening.

The sign of the pentagram is also sometimes used by individuals as a simple form of blessing. The fingers of the right hand are touched lightly to the center of the forehead, right breast, left shoulder, right shoulder, left breast, and forehead in turn.

Pagan
Lore

The Witches Rede of Chivalry

 nsofar as the Craft of the Wise is the most ancient and most honorable creed of humankind, it behooves all who are Witches to act in ways that give respect to the Old Gods, to their sisters and brothers of the Craft, and to themselves. Therefore, be it noted that:

1. Chivalry is a high code of honor which is of most ancient Pagan origin, and must be lived by all who follow the Old ways.

2. It must be kenned that thoughts and intent put forth on this Middle-Earth will wax strong in other worlds beyond, and return . . . bringing into creation, on this world, that which had been sent forth. Thus one should exercise discipline, for "as ye do plant, so shall ye harvest."

3. It is only by preparing our minds to be as Gods that we can ultimately attain godhead.

4. "This above all . . . . to thine own self be true . . . "

5. A Witch's word must have the validity of a signed and witnessed oath. Thus, give thy word sparingly, but adhere to it like iron.

6. Refrain from speaking ill of others, for not all truths of the matter may be known.

7. Pass not unverified words about another, for hearsay is, in large part, a thing of falsehoods.

8. Be thou honest with others, and have them known that honesty is likewise expected of them.

9. The fury of the moment plays folly with the truth; to keep one's head is a virtue.

10. Contemplate always the consequences of thine acts upon others. Strive not to harm.

11. Diverse covens may well have diverse views on love between members and with others. When a coven, clan, or grove is visited or joined, one should discern quietly their practices, and abide thereby.

12. Dignity, a gracious manner, and a good humor are much to be admired.

13. As a Witch, thou hast power, and thy powers wax strongly as wisdom increases. Therefore exercise discretion in the use thereof.

14. Courage and honor endure forever. Their echoes remain when the mountains have crumbled to dust.

15. Pledge friendship and fealty to those who so warrant. Strengthen others of the Brethren and they shall strengthen thee.

16. Thou shalt not reveal the secrets of another Witch or another Coven. Others have labored long and hard for

them, and cherish them as treasures.

17. Though there may be differences between those of the Old Ways, those who are once-born must see nothing, and must hear nothing.

18. Those who follow the mysteries should be above reproach in the eyes of the world.

19. The laws of the land should be obeyed whenever possible and within reason, for in the main they have been chosen with wisdom.

20. Have pride in thyself, and seek perfection in body and in mind. For the Lady has said, "How canst thou honor another unless thou give honor to thyself first?"

21. Those who seek the Mysteries should consider themselves as select of the Gods, for it is they who lead the race of humankind to the highest of thrones and beyond the very stars.

Forming a Pagan Training Group

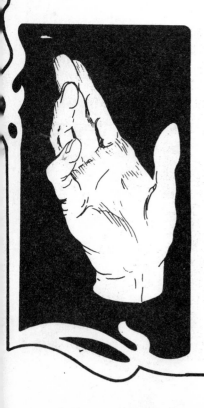

n today's Craft there seems to be an unfortunate lack of openings available in coven training groups. Although there are many sincere and devoted seekers of the Religion of the Goddess, local High Priests and Priestesses often find it very difficult to pull away from the mundane demands of everyday life to find the time to set aside for training new would-be initiates. It also happens that those living in out-of-the-way areas are frequently not able to work on a regular basis with accomplished Craft leaders. One other major aspect of the problem is that since coven groups are very small, tightly organized, close-knit units, potential initiates often do not blend in perfectly with the personality types of the other coven members. Thus, in order to preserve the family-like harmony which is so very vital to a coven unit, good and worthy people are turned down because it is simply not possible to find a place open that is "just right" for them. Sometimes there can be only one solution to these problems— if you want to train with a group, you just have to start your own group! We offer the following suggestions:

1.   **Overcoming the number 1 biggest problem in getting a training group off the ground: self-confidence in personal leadership abilities.** If there are no established group leaders, you will have to take the responsibilities upon yourself. This entails both making the necessary decisions and seeing to it that they are carried out. It is, of course, impossible to do this without confidence in yourself. Sometimes people new to the Craft feel very inhibited because they fear they do not as yet have very much knowledge, and they worry that taking on any sort of responsibilities might be considered presumptuous. Such a lack of knowledge should not be a hindrance when it is borne in mind that a coven works in an atmosphere of "perfect love" and "perfect trust." The other group members — in the spirit of love and friendship — are supportive, encouraging, understanding, and tolerant. (Note: if this does not typify your coven group, you are not true Witches, and you might as well disband immediately). It should also be remembered that OUR Gods have a sense of humor, so don't worry about bungling rituals occasionally. Furthermore, Craft-type knowledge tends to be "circular" rather than "linear." That is, it consists not of accumulated factual information, so much as basic theories and ideals which can be shared and experienced by a group. With this in mind, there is no reason to feel shy about taking the

initiative in getting your friends together to share in studying the occult mysteries of the Goddess.

2.   **Start out casually at first:** Once you have contacted a number of friends who seem enthusiastic about Craft working, you can organize some casual get-togethers, dinner parties, soirees, for the purpose of giving the group the opportunity to feel each other out about their respective attitudes toward the Craft and the level to which they are willing to commit themselves. This will also provide the opportunity to explore the common interests which the group shares, and the directions they wish to take in studying the occult and the Craft. It will be necessary to avoid putting any sort of pressure on individuals who seem uncertain and fearful of making such a commitment, often such individuals are uninformed about what Wiccancraft really is, and are expecting something entirely different than what Craft work means to you. In time, these persons will get to know the Craft better, and will be better able to determine whether this is the religion that they want to become involved in — but in the meanwhile, it is better not to force them into anything that they might have reservations about. It is also necessary to avoid involving persons who by nature have a very hysterical temperment — even very minor workings could be dangerous to the neurotic and over-imaginative person. In starting out, it is necessary to take things slow and easy, maintaining a comfortable casual atmosphere.

3.   **A very easy approach to take in starting out is to experiment with ESP exercises in the form of parlor games:** There are many possible games and exercises which will not only develop psychic ability, but will also serve to help the group to relax, enjoy themselves, and get to know each other better. One of the most common is to test telepathic ability by playing with the Rhine cards, the familiar deck of squares, triangles, circles, etc. A fun way to test psychometric ability is to collect photographs which have strong emotional or elemental connotations — such as a wedding photo, a family pet, wind blowing in the trees, a thunderstorm over the lake, etc. and insert them into heavy envelopes. Each member of the group can contribute a couple of pictures for this purpose. Then individual envelopes are traded as members of the group attempt to pull impressions off of them, actually trying to "guess" what sort of picture is in the envelope. All sorts of games involving divination, pendulum, tarot, etc., can be both enjoyable and educational. The various members of the group

will be able to use their imaginations to devise many other entertaining experiments to exercise and test the psychic powers.

4. **Meditative exercises are a very excellent means to opening psychic centers, and at the same time developing a closer group rapport:** It is well to begin every meeting with a quiet period of meditation. For example, your group may wish to link hands, synchronize their breathing, and place their minds in a subjective state, while at the same time concentrating on pulling cosmic power in and out through the pores of the body and especially directing it to the psychic centers. Meditations can also involve listening to music, concentrating on special symbols (such as tarot cards or astrological symbolism), contemplating beautiful poems or names of Power, and so on.

5. **Research and Reading Assignments:** Readings and critiques of popular books written about the Craft, Occult, and other related subjects are valuable in stimulating the exchange of ideas, and also in revealing the respective attitudes and positions of each group member. Sometimes it will be desirable to request each person to present a brief, inspirational reading to the group, as part of a meditation. For this purpose, research into mythology is very useful.

However, in this case, the critique of books is designed to stimulate lively discussions. A training coven should by all means avoid using the precious time that they have together to study subjects that the individuals could simply read about on their own time. Because most people are not able to get together very often, group time should be spent on activities and experiments wherein working together is required. For example, if the subject is telepathy, members should read about it to gain factual information beforehand, and then group time should be used to carry out actual experiments in telepathy, something which requires cooperative participation. When people commit themselves to working together in a training group, every moment has to count.

An additional note about reading assignments is that it is more desirable to read the "right" books instead of the "wrong" books. Therefore, it is necessary to have at least one member of the group who can provide bibliographies of valid and reputable reading materials.

6. **Basic Circle Workings:** The spiritual aspects of the Wicca religion are very important in the coven training

group, and it will not be long before members are eager to try working some basic rituals, especially at Full Moons and high sabbats. It is becoming much easier for people new to the Craft to get hold of rituals that are generalized, light, and uncomplicated. The Pagan Way rituals and the basic rites of the Outer Court were especially designed for such purposes, and can be easily altered and adapted to suit individual needs and personalities of differing covens. There are, in addition, many fine books and magazines such as the "Crystal Well" which cater to the Pagan-Wiccan community in providing ritual material.*

Neophytes should definitely not feel self-conscious about performing Craft rituals, for the reasons stated before. Rituals of a light and casual nature should be performed at first, however, the important thing is that the spirit of the ritual occasion is observed. At the same time, it is necessary to maintain a reverential attitude and work for tight circle discipline. Talking, giggling, interrupting, insulting, and other forms of rudeness while a ritual is being conducted are certain guarantees of failure.

It might be mentioned, in addition, that many covens prefer not to mix magical workings with religious worship; some use weekly esbats to accomplish magical business of a mundane nature, and reserve the eight festival sabbats, and often the Full Moons, for striving for accomplishments of a higher spiritual nature.

7.   Making Hypnosuggestive Techniques Work for You: As an evening session is preparing to close, there are certain very simple techniques making use of the power of suggestion, which can be used to aid in the accomplishment of things the group considers important. Such suggestion is most effectively applied when the group is in a state of relaxation or meditation. The possibilities where hypno-suggestion can be put to use are innumerable. For example, group members may wish to develop clairvoyance: during the evening meditation, each individual will place his/her mind in a very subjective state while one person speaks to the rest, telling them that as they relax and breathe deeply, their third eyes begin to tingle and become more sensitive. In addition, they are told that as they return home that night to go to bed, the darkness will only heighten and reinforce

*The Crystal Well has suspended publication for an indefinite period, although Circle Network News (Box 219, Mt. Horeb, WI 53672) is highly recommended for background information, Wicca and Pagan open meeting schedules, and contacts.

their ability to perceive psychic energy, auras, etc. As another example, the group could have one person plant the suggestion in their minds that when they fall asleep, they will have vivid dreams in which they will meet with the rest of the group members, and converse with beings from higher planes, gaining knowledge of spiritual importance. Forms of suggestion can be used toward any number of other accomplishments, anthing from losing weight, to dream control, to developing greater psychic sensitivities. In essence, what you are doing is making your unconscious mind work for you. The sooner one is able to turn in to sleep, the stronger the suggestion will remain in the subconsicous, especially when the desired working involves some form of dream control. The reason for reserving work with suggestion until the close of the meeting is that as the last order of business, the mind can work on it with less distraction.

8.   **Beware of Psychic Freeloading:** As a coven becomes more proficient in psychic and magical workings, one of the annoyances which it soon learns about, is that a constant stream of people will start beating a path to its door with all kinds of problems to be magically solved. You will never lack for magical tasks to work on. Everyone will have friends, relatives, neighbors, casual acquaintances, etc., with problems.

Furthermore, it is an unfortunate fact that many individuals are attracted to coven membership because they have many personal problems and they hope that by joining a group, they will have a large number of people solving their troubles by constantly doing magic for them. Such persons are able to invent a thousand ways of wasting the group's energy, which is another good reason for selective membership and careful screening of applicants. Eventually, it becomes necessary to set priorities on the kinds of work to be done, and many requests for help may have to be turned down. The fact is. the individual Witch also has a responsibility to keep her/himself healthy, and cannot allow personal energy to be frittered away by minor magical tasks. It can be difficult enough to build up and store energy, so it should only be directed toward workings of major importance.

RUNES OF IMPORTANCE

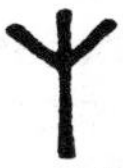 MAN

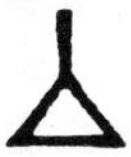 WOMAN

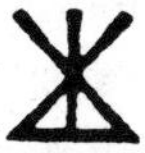 LOVE

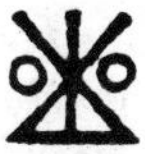 FAMILY or clan

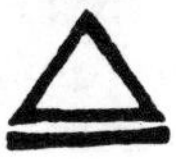 the HOME

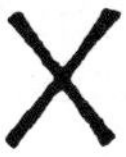 GIFTS—legacies, promotions, windfalls

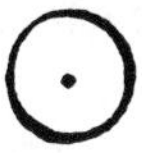 MONEY—material gain, financial concerns

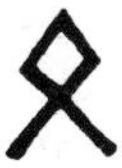 POSSESSIONS—tangible 'things' or mental & spiritual attributes

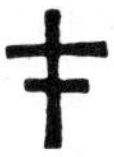 POISON—gossip, slander, negativity, 'Bad Vibes'

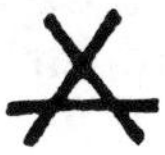 DISORDERED THOUGHTS—emotional tension, irrationality, etc.

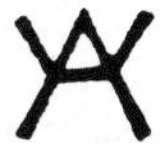 WAR—any conflict or quarrels

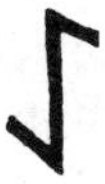 DEATH—usually means 'end of the matter' but can actually mean physical death

 COMFORT—pleasure, ease, security, happiness

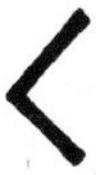 FIRE—adds the traditional associates of fire to stones near it

Notes from the Outer Court Book of Shadows

he Outer Court Book of Shadows is a good-sized compilation of rituals, spells, witch traditions, and miscellaneous "how to" instructions. Originally designed as a fully self-contained *training* system for Gardnerian Wicca, the outer court has since spread on its own as an independent tradition, and has been modified into quite a few different versions. Ed Fitch pulled together fragments of ancient ritual, literature, and spells from the Celtic lands, Eastern Europe, and ancient Greece, then restored them along a basic Gardnerian format. Others have since added more material. Like nearly all Books of Shadows, this volume (plus a companion tome of magical training, the *Grimoire of the Shadows*) is usually privately copied and passed from one group to another. There are many of these "underground classics" about, though very few of them have been in open publication.

THE GODS OF THE CRAFT
Level 1.
Absolute Godhood — the level of transcendence, Gnosis (Knowledge of Godhood).
Level 2.
The Harmonious and Creative Duality of the God and Goddess; at this level the Absolute is objectified in its application to the masculine and feminine forces in Nature.
Level 3.
The Archetypes; bringing the gods to the human sphere, at this level Godhead attains will and intelligence. To this level belong the gods and goddesses which are worshipped by the worldly religions.

RELATIONS OF THE ARCHETYPES
Because there is such a diversity of Wiccan systems in America, different groups place a differing emphasis on the varying archetypical relationships in their personal seasonal rites and Craft mythology, although all of these relationships are important to the myths of the Craft. Here are the most basic combinations:

DUALISTIC RELATIONSHIP: The God and Goddess relate to each other as brother-sister, husband-wife. Familiar examples from the mythology of the world include the Greek/Roman Deus-pater and Deus-mater, (Zeus/Jupiter and Hera/Juno/Demeter), Fauna and Faunus, Diana-Lucina and Dianus-Apollo, etc., and the Teutonic "Vanir" gods Freya and Freyr, and Njord and

Nerthus. This relationship bears resemblance to the Yin-Yang concept of Chinese religion. This system is especially important to the Gardnerian version of the Craft.

TRIADIC RELATIONSHIP OF MOTHER, FATHER, AND CHILD: Examples include the Egyptian Isis-Osiris Horus; the Greek/Roman Demeter-Zeus-Dionysius or Demeter-Zeus-Persephone, the Italian Diana-Lucifer-Aradia; and the Celtic Rhiannon-Pwyll-Pryderi. A modified version of this relationship is found in the Catholic religion.

TRIPLE FACE OF THE GODDESS (DEA TRIFORMIS): Representing Her Aspects as Maiden, Mother, and Crone: Examples include the Greek/Roman Persephone-Demeter and the hag Demeter at Eleusis, Seine-Luna-Hecate; the Celtic Matronase and the triple Goddess Bride; and the Goddess personification receives particular emphasis in the Craft, which is largely Celtic, and has gained special vitality through the representations of the Triple Goddess in Robert Graves' book, *The White Goddess.* **Dual Nature of the God as King of the Waxing Year and King of the Waning Year.** In some cases this is developed into a triad, where the two gods are seen as twin brothers, one light, the other dark, contending for the hand of the Goddess, and in other cases there is a father-son relationship where the child becomes the Divine King, only to wane with the coming winter and be succeeded by his son and rival. Examples include the Greek Prometheus-Epimetheus; the Egyptian Set-Osiris; the Near Eastern Baal-Mat; the Celtic Lugh-Balor; and the Teutonic, Hoder-Balder. Emphasis on this relationship has also been popularized by the noted poet and author, Robert Graves.

These are some of the major distinctions in God-Goddess relationships. There are many additional variations on these basic relationships.

Neopagans also borrow from the mythologies of many lands when they want to work with a specific archetypal form. For example, an individual wishing to work with the Godforce personifying Wisdom, may choose to work with either Athena, Hermes, or Thoth; an individual wishing to explore the erotic aspect of the Godforce may consult Aphrodite/Venus or Pan, and so on.

In the sense that Wiccans work with so many different archetypal forms, they are said to have a "polytheistic" religion.

NOTE: So extensive is the subject of myths, gods, and archetypes, that the Outer Court Book has not the space to deal with explanations of these. For an understanding of archetypal images, the student is urged to resort to the works of Carl Jung and his followers. The study of ancient myths is also essential to the student of the Craft, as our roots lie in these old legends.

AN ADDITIONAL WORD ON MYTH: In addition to identifying the archetypal images in myth, we take a "Gestalt" approach as well. Myth is viewed as the Sacred Drama of the archetypes, and the individual who properly understands a myth actually experiences and lives the message of the myth, gaining an uplifting insight into the mysteries of Nature and Godhood.

PERSONAL RELIGIONS

Neopagans are able to recognize these differing levels of Godhood. They work in magic and ritual with the part of the human psyche and come closest to human understanding. At the same time, the Pagan believes that it is perfectly possible to keep one's feet "firmly on the ground," while at the same time striving for the transcendental attainment of the Absolute or realization of the Gnosis. The Wiccan holds that the Knowledge of God is found within one's own being, when one lives in a state of Perfect Love and Perfect Harmony with the forces of the Universe. To coin a phrase, "Thou are God."

Wiccan groups differ in the way they view the God and Goddess forces. Today it is very common for covens to be very "matrifocal," emphasizing the worship of the Goddess in the religion. Some groups, referred to as "Dianic" covens, omit the role of the God entirely and admit only females into membership. This unbalance is a reaction to the very heavily "patrifocal" emphasis that our society's dominant religions have taken. In more archaic times, there was probably more of a balance between the masculine and feminine aspects of the Craft. This Outer Court Book takes a matrifocal stance (1) because we feel that at this point in time a heavy emphasis on the feminine is needed to balance out society's heavy emphasis on the masculine; and (2) because we feel that the human emotions relate better to objectifying the Absolute in its soft, warm, nurturing aspect.

Delving back into the archaic Pagan roots of Wicca, scholars differ over theories pertaining to the God-Goddess relationship. Some believe that the God was predominant at first when hunting and gathering was the earliest mode of subsistence, and that the Goddess came to predominance later with the introduction of agriculture. Others say that the Goddess was originally predominant, stating that the maternal role was more obvious and important than the paternal. However, this Outer Court holds that early humans were able to recognize the harmonious duality of male and female from the very beginning, and that equality in the God-Goddess relationship is the most archaic form.

MONISM and PANTHEISM vs. DUALISM

Wiccancraft, along with most true Western Pagan theologies, is a "monistic" religion. This means that Wiccans view Godhood as being at one with all Nature, unlike some other religions which are "dualistic," believing that man and Nature are corrupt and separate from God, and that the goal of man is to escape from life, the world, and even the "Self" identity. Dualistic religions view the world as a vale of tears, and emphasize the suffering and negativity in life. Wiccans, on the other hand, realize that there is indeed a negative side to existence and the material world, but they believe that evil can be surmounted by maintaining a positive outlook and realizing humanity's divine nature. (The Christian devil, incidentally, is also part of a dualistic concept, and as such has nothing whatsoever to do with the Wiccan religion, contrary to many false conceptions). When Wiccans do use the term "duality" in their religious beliefs, they are referring to the creative, harmonious, and complementary duality of male and female, rather than the sharp dichotomy between good and evil which dualistic religions make.

Another word describing the Wiccan religion is "pantheistic," meaning "God in everything." According to this belief, all of nature — every particle of energy and every piece of matter — contains a spark of the Divine. Thus, the Pagan endeavors to be in tune with the forces and rhythms of nature in order to broaden wisdom and understanding. Contrary to what some irresponsible scholars have said, Pagans do not bow down and worship the Sun and the Moon and other natural phenomena. What this does mean, is that we can see the nature of Divinity symbolically manifest in these.

Familiar Household Pets

f you have a couple of pets around your house, and you think that you would like to help them to start developing their innate magical abilities and at the same time increasing your own psychic rapport with them — then how about beginning their psychic training program right now! There's no time to lose, and you can probably start getting results immediately!

Listed here are a number of tests and exercises you can run your animals through whenever you can find a spare moment. You can also try these experiments out with the pets of friends and strangers.

1. **Establishing a basic mental rapport and telepathic contact.** A very simple and common exercise can be tried: sit across the room from an animal with which you wish to experiment. Relax yourself as you focus your attention on the pet, mentally conveying to it the desire that it should get up and come over to you. Try doing this both with and without eye contact. A variation on this is rather than conveying a mental message, try to project an emotional message. Form a great big chunk of positive love energy, and send it over to the animal, observing the effects which it may have. With a little proficiency, these exercises may also be used to attract wild animals.

A reversal of this exercise is to use telepathic powers to scare an animal off, or simply to send it away. Another interesting technique is to project a mental image of yourself, perhaps as a large ferocious beast. The important thing, of course, is not to show any fear yourself, as an animal can sense this, and your projections will not be effective.

2. **Charged Energy Transmission.** In a manner much similar to establishing telepathic contacts, you can experiment with various forms of building up energy and directing it toward an animal. Approach the animal as it is calm and relaxed, and use your favorite means of transferring psychic energy. For example, after basic energy pore-breathing,* release stored energy through your hands as you stroke the animal, or transfer the energy through eye-to-eye contact. Take note of the degree to which the animal becomes more active. The purpose of such an exercise is its use as a basis to healing, especially healing magic which involves sending a heavy charge of psychic energy to "boost" the strength. A variation of this is to direct the energy charge to a

*See page 87.

specific area of the body, for example, trying to speed up recovery in an animal which has a broken leg or a sore throat. Also experiment with directing energy in patterns to stimulate sensitive areas (such as over the chakras) as a type of "psychic massage." These techniques can certainly be applied to humans as well, after you have practiced and perfected them on your pets.

Familiars often enjoy being present at circle rites because of the large amounts of power built up. By carefully paying attention to the nature of your pet's reactions on such occasions, you can use him as a meter to the level of intensity of the energy raised.

3. **Relaxing, Calming** you can test your own psychic abilities by attempting to calm and soothe an animal which is tense, nervous, or simply in a very active mood. A large part of this technique consists of projecting soothing emotions and calming telepathic messages. Experiment with methods of transferring power which actually employ energy to relax specific areas. Use physical contact, stroking, massaging, etc. Make careful observations of how reactions differ when 1) only physical contact is used; 2) when there is no physical contact but telepathic techniques are used; and 3) when psychic techniques are combined with physical methods. Relaxation exercises such as these are also used as a basis to healing.

4. **Pet's Reaction to Emotional Moods** in order to get a general assessment of your pet's degree of perceptiveness, take careful notes on the animal's reaction to the emotional climate. Does the pet tend to have certain different reactions when exposed to general moods of joy, elation, anger, hostility, tension, etc.? Try to project some of these feelings yourself and test the reactions.

5. **Pet's Interactions with Other Animals.** It can be a lot of fun to watch how your familiar communicates with other animals. How do they seem to interact? Do you think there's any possibility of telepathic and other paranormal means of communication in addition to the usual physical signals that animals use? Closely note whether there is any difference in the communication techniques of trained familiars as opposed to ordinary animals.

6. **Artificial Elementals.** Another method of testing perception, and at the same time exercising your own abilities, is experimentation with your pet's reactions and interactions with artificial elementals. An "artificial elemental" is a living entity of energy which you yourself

can create. Such a being may take on an intelligence of its own, or it may be no more than a bubble of energy. It may come alive for only a second, or it may live for years. It is possible to make such an entity by pouring energy into an inanimate object, imbuing it with life force. To make the point clearer, I must relate some of our own experiments with this. One of my oldest "pets" is a little red rubber ball which long ago I made into a tiny imp. My favorite is a toy fox which has been my companion on many adventures. It seems that whenever I take Inishkea (my fox) to visit someone who owns dogs, it is all we can do to keep the dogs off of him. It seems, somehow, that the antipathy between fox and dog exists even on a psychic level. A most unusual thing took place once at a friend's house. The subject of artificial elementals was brought up, and at that moment I thought about my little fox which I had left at home. Suddenly my friend's dog got up from where he had been resting and began to jump all over me, acting in a very wild manner. My own three cats have very ambiguous feelings toward Inishkea, acting somewhat fearful of him — although "Butchi," our little amazon female, occasionally hunts him and tries to carry him off. Ordinarily stuffed toys don't seem to interest the cats. Once we decided to see what the cats would do if we turned some baby toys into temporary elemental beings. First we instilled an energy charge into a yellow duckie; at the same time projecting very light-hearted bouncy duckie feelings and images. The cats immediately became very interested in catching the duckie, and trying to drag it off as their kill. Then we took a pink bunny, but as we poured energy into it, we instilled it with projections of a very monstrous, formidable kind, sort of a Frankenstein bunny. When the cats saw it, they ran away, and although we left it lying there, they wouldn't go near it. It was particularly interesting for us to test the degree of the cats' reactions: Emilie, in many ways the most sensitive, acted the most skittish, whereas Niki "Fatty Catty" who is about as psychically sensitive as a brick, appeared the least disturbed by the strange creature. These are just some examples of the fun you can have when you are playing with your familiars. In fact, artificial elementals can make rather good pets themselves, and you can program them to work on simple magical tasks for you.

7.   **Shapeshifting.** A unique new way of playing with your pet involves shapeshifting. Project your consciousness out of your body, detaching yourself from physical

awareness, and visualize yourself in the form of another animal. In this "astral" form, try to accompany your pet on its adventures.

8. **Projection of Consciousness.** In order to see the world from a new perspective, try "getting under" your familiar's skin. Under the proper conditions of relaxation, and with strong capacities for visualization and concentration, you can project your consciousness into the mind of your pet. First of all, you must isolate your own self awareness from your physical body. Then focusing your attention on the animal, visualize yourself seeing as the animal sees, feeling all of the sensations which it is able to experience. On a basic level, this exercise is good for developing concentration. With greater adeptness, such an ability opens new realms of experience and expands the individual consciousness in perceiving the world around you.

The techniques are simplified for basic use at any time. Most of these methods are of the sort which actually develop your own innate abilities in addition to testing the perception of the pet. With all of these exercises, there is potential for greater development and more sophisticated use.

TO THE SUN

Greetings to you, Sun of the season,
As you travel the skies on high,
With your strong steps on the
        wing of the heights;
You are the happy Mother of the Stars.

You sink down in the perilous ocean
Without harm and without hurt;
You rise up on the quiet wave
Like a young queen in flower.

TO THE NEW MOON

Greetings to you, New Moon,
Kindly jewel of guidance!
I bend my knees to you,
I offer you my love.

I bend my knees to you,
I raise my hands to you,
I lift up my eye to you,
New Moon of the Seasons.

Greetings to you, New Moon,
Darling of my love!
Greetings to you, New Moon,
Darling of the Graces.

You journey on your course,
You steer the flood-tides,
You lift up your face for us,
New Moon of the seasons.

Queen of guidance,
Queen of good luck,
Queen of my love,
New Moon of the Seasons!

Seasonal
Rites

Spring Rite

he place of the rite should be decked with flowers, green boughs, colored ribbons about trees and bushes, brightly decorated eggs, and other decorations of the season. At the center of the ritual area shall be a cauldron which contains some cold, pure water. (Just before the rite a piece of dry ice may be added for effect.) About the cauldron shall be placed thirteen candles of various colors to be lit at the start of the ceremony. Sweet incense (rose, strawberry, jasmine, or such) should be lit before the rite and renewed frequently. At each quarter, just at the edge of the ritual area, shall be placed a cluster of three white candles, to be lit during the rite. If the ritual is to be held in open air, the candles should be placed within glass jars to shield them from the wind. Also, each cluster of quarter candles may be replaced by a torch.

(It should be noted, of course, that this rite is not to be taken as an unchangeable rede. Each group can and should modify it to fit their own needs.)

All partaking of the rite should be clad in ceremonial robes or Pagan-like costumes of white or of light colors if possible. Flowers and leafy garlands should be worn in the hair. Pagan or nature-oriented jewelry is most appropriate at this time.

Light, sweet cakes should be baked — honeycakes are traditional — one for each in the rite plus one additional to be dedicated to the Lady. The cakes should be placed on a plate next to the cauldron. Also, boiled and decorated eggs (one per person plus one to be dedicated to the Lady—) and some milk for each in the ritual plus appropriate cups or goblets.

When all is in readiness, the Priest should summon all to silently gather about in a circle around the cauldron and link hands. The Priestess lights the candles about the cauldron, then stands and says:

Seekers of the ancient ways, think upon
The coming again of the warm seasons.
Of the return of life.
And of the ways in which our distant ancestors
Once honored the Old Gods
And gave blessings to field and forest
In times far past.

There shall be a pause for silent meditation of not less than twenty-five heartbeats. Then the Priestess shall say:

We now celebrate the awakening of the Earth
And the return of beauty and of fruitfulness.
Life has quickened forest, meadow, and field.
Let us celebrate the return of the gentle times
With spell and chant and song.
Let the far kingdoms be hailed!

The one chosen to be the Caller of the Winds shall take the incense censer and go to the East to light the flames there. Then shall the Caller hold forth the incense, calling:

Soft and whispering winds from afar,
Greetings be unto thee
In the Names of the Old Gods.
Blow clear and fresh and free.
In magickal presence here.
Blessed Be!
All: BLESSED BE!

The one chosen to be the Caller of the Light shall take the incense censer and go to the South to light the flames there. Then the Caller shall hold forth the incense, invoking:

Warming and quickening light from afar,
Greetings be unto thee
In the Names of the Old Gods.
Grant the warmth that brings forth life.
In magickal presence here.
Blessed Be!
All: BLESSED BE!

The one chosen to be the Caller of the Waters shall take the incense censer and go to the West to light the flames there. Then shall the Caller hold forth the incense, invoking:

Cool waters of lake and of stream,
Greetings be unto thee
In the Names of the old Gods.
Flow clear and pure and swift.
In Magickal presence here.
Blessed Be!
All: BLESSED BE!

The one chosen to be the Caller of the lands shall take the incense censer and go to the North to light the flames there. Then shall the Caller hold forth the incense, invoking:

> *Far lands and wild places,*
> *Greetings be unto thee.*
> *In the Names of the Old Gods.*
> *Awaken from your sleep*
> *To bring forth bounty.*
> *In magickal presence here.*
> *Blessed Be!*

All: BLESSED BE!

The incense censer is silently offered up at the eastern quarter and replaced by the cauldron. The Priest raises his arms in salute, calling:

> *We give you greetings*
> *O laughing Lord of the Greenwood,*
> *Guardian of the wild things,*
> *Friend and protector of those who*
> *Seek the wilderness.*
> *Grant here your joyous, potent, and enlivening*
>   *presence.*
> *Enjoy our rite as do we,*
> *And grant us of your lust*
> *For beauty and for life.*
> *Blessed Be!*

All: BLESSED BE!

The priestess raises her arms in salute, calling:

> *We give you greetings,*
> *O loving and gracious Lady of the Earth,*
> *Patroness of the field and of meadow,*
> *Queen of forest and of stream,*
> *Giving love, passion, and beauty.*
> *Grant here your gentle, laughing*
> *And magickal presence.*
> *Enjoy our rite as do we,*
> *And grant us of your power to enchant*
> *And to create.*
> *Blessed Be!*

All: BLESSED BE!

The Priest then says:

> *At this time and in this place*
> *We now call forth and give honor*

To the seasons of life and of fresh beginnings.
It is a time for all which is good,
For all beings which are new and small,
And of promise for the future.

The Priestess then says:

At this time and in this place
To the seasons of life and of fresh beginnings.
It is a time for all which is good,
For all beings which are new and small,
And of promise for the future.

Then the Priestess says:

At this time and in this place
Do we salute our noble Goddess
As the Sacred Maiden
Now returned from cold and from darkness
To spread forth Her blessings
Upon the reborn lands.

The Priest then says to all:

Let us now call upon
The life returning everywhere anew.
Call now as I do call!
COME FORTH, O LIVING WATERS!*
COME FORTH, O LIFE-GIVING
    EARTH!*
COME FORTH, O SOFT RAINS!*
COME FORTH, O GENTLE WINDS!*
COME FORTH, O WARMTH OF
    THE SUN!*

There shall be a pause of five heartbeats. Then shall the
Priest continue:

BLESSED BE FIELDS!*
BLESSED BE FORESTS!*
BLESSED BE THE
    LAKES AND THE STREAMS!*
BLESSED BE THE GREAT POWERS
    OF LIFE!*
BLESSED BE THE NOBLE GODDESS!*
BLESSED BE THE LAUGHING GOD!*

*All repeat.

The Priest then says to all:

> *Link hands all.*
> *Let us repeat the ancient chant*
> *As we build and send forth*
> *The Power of the natural world.*

All link hands and begin a dancing procession deosil (clockwise) with the Priestess and Priest leading by chanting and dancing swiftly deosil within the circle. All shall repeat the following chant:

> *ERCE, ERCE, ERCE.*
> *HAIL EARTH,*
> *MOTHER OF ALL!*

The procession, the dance, and the chant shall be continued for so long as the Priest/Priestess deem necessary. Then the Priest shall call:

> *All cease!*
> *Turn!*
> *And direct the Power we have built*
> *Into the sacramental cakes,*
> *The eggs of the season*
> *And the sacred milk*
> *Beside the cauldron!*

All shall drop to their knees or to a sitting position abruptly, arms outstreached towards the honey-cakes, eggs, and milk beside the cauldron, and remain thus in silence for a period of twenty-five heartbeats. Then shall the Priestess say:

> *The Power we have gathered*
> *Is imbued within these sweet cakes,*
> *The eggs and milk of life.*
> *Granting us strength, health, fortune*
> *So the Power also goes forth*
> *So that the land be fertile*
> *And all creatures prosper.*
> *In the Name of the most excellent Goddess*
> *And Her sturdy Consort.*
> *So mote it be!*

All: SO MOTE IT BE!

The Priestess and the Priest shall then take the cakes and pass them to those within the ritual area, the Priestess serving the men and the Priest serving the women. Each is given a cake, an egg, and poured milk, with the salutation:

> *The blessings*
> *Of the Old Ones*
> *Be with you.*

Each should eat of the cake and break off parts to give to others about, and similarly share eggs and milk. The cake intended as an offering to the Lady shall be broken and placed beneath trees and shrubs; the egg that is offered should be buried beneath a plant. (If the rite is done indoors, this may be done afterwards.)

Other seasonally appropriate workings or other activities may be accomplished at this time, such as dancing, power chants, singing, sharing of wine, and so on.

When she feels that it is time to conclude the ritual, the Priestess shall raise her arms for silence and say to all:

> *Friends, at this time*
> *We end this ritual of spring.*
> *We have given the proper salutation*
> *And become close to the seasonal Forces*
> *And close to the old ways of magic.*
> *Callers of the Far Kingdoms,*
> *Give now our farewells.*

The one chosen to be the Caller of the Winds shall take the censer of incense and go to the East. Incense shall be offered and the flames there put out, saying:

> *Soft and whispering winds from afar,*
> *We thank you, and give our blessings*
> *To thy far realms.*
> *Blessed Be!*
> *All:* BLESSED BE!

The one chosen to be the Caller of the Light shall take the incense censer and go to the South. Incense shall be offered and the flames there put out, saying:

> *Warming and quickening light from afar,*
> *We thank you, and give our blessings*
> *to thy far realms.*
> *Blessed Be!*
> *All:* BLESSED BE!

The one chosen to be the Caller of the Waters shall take the censer of incense and go to the West. Incense shall be offered and the flames there put out, saying:

> *Cool waters of lake and of stream,*
> *We thank you, and give our blessings*
> *To thy far realms.*
> *Blessed Be!*

All: BLESSED BE!

The one chosen to be the Caller of the Lands shall take the incense censer and go to the North. Incense shall be offered and the flames there put out, saying:

> *Far lands and wild places,*
> *We thank you, and give our blessings*
> *To ty far realms.*
> *Blessed Be!*

All: BLESSED BE!

Incense is silently offered up at the eastern quarter and the censer replaced by the cauldron. The Priest holds forth his hands in salute, calling:

> *O laughing Lord of the Greenwood,*
> *We thank thee for thy powerful presence here.*
> *We have been honored to have your spirit*
> *Here among us.*
> *Hail, farewell, and blessed be!*

All: HAIL, FAREWELL, AND BLESSED BE!

The Priestess holds up her hands in salute and calls:

> *O loving and gracious Lady of the Earth,*
> *We thank thee for thy enchanting presence here.*
> *We have been honored to have your spirit*
> *Here among us.*
> *Hail, farewell, and blessed be!*

All: HAIL, FAREWELL, AND BLESSED BE!

The Priestess puts out the candles about the cauldron, leaving perhaps five or eight to burn for the rest of the evening if so desired. She then says:

The Goddess and the God
And the Earth itself
Have been honored
This rite of spring is done.
Merry meet and merry part.

After this rite, the water from the cauldron should be poured on the plants and shrubs.

ABOUT THE SPRING RITE

This is a free-flowing celebration of the return of spring and the reawakening of life from the earth as it would have been done in northern Europe in ancient Pagan times, when the forests were dense and all lived close to the land. The calling upon the earth, the winds, the sun and the streams . . . as well as milk, eggs, and sweet cakes in tasty and imaginative versions . . . is typical of that long era. The chant, "Erce, Erce, Erce,/Hail Earth/Mother of All" (Erce is pronounced "ur-kay") was used in the pre-Medieval German lands and may still be a backwoods spell in that country today.

Midsummer Rite

This ritual marks the turning of the year from waxing to waning, and was celebrated in many parts of ancient Europe. While traditionally a time of festival, it is in its deeper aspects, a time for pausing and viewing the more profound meanings of mid-earth existence as perceived by the Witch and the Pagan. Hence, this is one rite which is to be shadowy, theatrical, and above all, a dramatic ceremony!

The area of the ritual should be set with a cauldron at the center, inside which a fire is to be kindled. Five various Stations of the Oracles are to be set up in five different directions from the cauldron center-point. If the rite is held out-of-doors, as would be best, then these Stations may be at a distance. If within, then they should be as far as possible from the center, and approached during the rite by a circuitous or maze-like route.

For this ritual, five masks should be made, using as inspiration the masks of the Sacred Theatre in ancient Greece. They may be simple, or they may be as ornate as the coven members desire. The masks should depict the Maiden, the Young King, the Lady, the Declining King, and the Crone, respectively. The intent is to represent the Divine Beings totally and in an archaic way, without the appearance or personalities of the speakers.

A mask should be hung on a pole perhaps five feet high at each Place of the Oracle, and a candle set before it, to be lit just before the rite. Incense sticks should also be placed by each pole. Each station should be set as a small shrine, and if possible be hidden until closely approached by the coven. And each mask should hang as if worn by an invisible being. Various members of the coven should have been chosen to represent each of the Great Ones and ideally (though not necessarily) have completely memorized the lines.

The Priestess and Priest shall see that all is in readiness. Candles are lit before each Station of the Oracle (within glass jars if outside, to protect them from the wind). A fire is lit within the cauldron, along with incense, at the center.

Then shall they call all members of the coven to gather around the cauldron, to explain the meaning of this season, and to describe how the festival was once celebrated by bonfires, by feasting, by coronation of the sacred king in some lands and by his symbolic death in other lands. A period of quiet meditation shall follow, wherein all shall consider what has been said.

The Priest shall light the candles or torches, then go before the cauldron and raising high his staff, call:

Great One of Heaven, power of the Sun,
We give honor to you,
And call upon you in your ancient Names:
Michael, Balin, Phol, Hugh, Herne,
Heimdul, Balder, Arthur, Perkunis...
We call upon you, friend of
Times far ancient.
Evoe Deus!
All: EVOE DEUS!

The Priestess shall then go before the cauldron and, raising high her staff, call:

Great One of the Stars, spinner of fates,
We give honor to you,
And call upon you in your ancient Names:
Fortuna, Aphrodite, Huldana, Mari,
Freya, Oestra, Morrigan, Cerridwen...
We call upon you, friend of
Times far ancient.
Evoe bona dea!
All: EVOE BONA DEA!

In silence shall the Priestess and Priest lead the group in a circuitous way, perhaps following a pre-planned maze, to the First Station. There all shall gather before the mask of the Maiden. The Priestess shall light incense, and hold incense and flame aloft for a few moments before the mask. Then shall the one chosen to speak for the Maiden go from the coven, stand behind the mask, and hold it before her face, saying:

Life springs eternal, with joy and with beauty.
Now is the time for celebration
Of the powers of life and of sensuousness,
Of newness and of richness,
For richness and plenty
Do bless all the lands.
Now shall be crowned the shining
Sacred King,
In the full knowledge that
All which is good, and pleasing,
Shall ever return, as glorious as before,
As certainly as the coming
Of the New Moon.

There shall be a pause of perhaps five heartbeats. If the Oracle feels inspired of the Maid, she may speak more, then replace the mask in its place and return to the coven.

Proceed as before to the Station of the Young King:

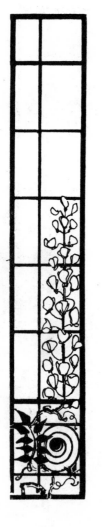

There is a time for all things to grow.
A time to build, and a time to explore.
A time for building empires,
And a time for laughing at the storm.
A time for exultation for the glory of the world,
And joy in one's own strength.
This is the time for celebration
Of the virile and bold season.
Now, with gladness, shall be crowned
The beauteous Sacred Queen,
In the full knowledge that times of joy
Shall return always, as lusty as before,
As certainly as the Sun
Shall rise again.

There shall be a pause of perhaps five heartbeats. If the Oracle feels inspired of the Young King, he may speak more, then replace the mask in its place and return to the coven.

Proceed as before, to the Station of the Lady:

As surely as the Moon becomes full,
All must ripen at last, seek its destiny,
And decline. Here it is that
The proud banners are planted,
The rich cities shine in their
Heights of splendour.
One at last sees and at last fully knows
The World, the Gods, and one's own soul.
Whatever thence happens, or however,
Be it of a vast nation, or within
The breast of one alone and solitary,
A point has been made
Before Eternity itself.
And so shall it remain
Forever.

There shall be a pause of perhaps five heartbeats. If the Oracle feels inspired of the Lady, she may speak more, then replace the mask in its place and return to the coven.

Proceed as before, to the Station of the Declining

King:

The Sun must set
And its light fade.
In the scheme of all things
There is a place for decline,
A time for ending affairs,
For the closing of doors,
For the razing of cities,
And the breaking of monuments.
For how can there be new life,
Unless death makes clear the way
And removes that which is old and outworn?
Know well that ending is as necessary
In all things, as is beginning,
And that there must be death
That ye may in time become as Gods
And, in your Quest,
Gain life eternal!

There shall be a pause of perhaps five heartbeats. If the Oracle feels inspired of the Declining King he may speak more, then replace the mask in its place and return to the coven.

Proceed as before, to the Station of the Crone:

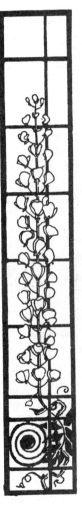

The Moon must decline, darken,
And die.
Beyond life are the realms of Shadow,
The journeys unknown and the visions undreamed.
For the soul seeks its own level, rests,
And gains a time and a place
To be reborn again.
Yet here also, between the worlds
Is wisdom deep and power great
That those who are fitting,
In mind and in spirit, may learn.
Ye who are worthy, seek this chalice of intellect
Of attainment, of magic.
Use it for your good, and the good of others.
For so shall ye gain, in time,
The power and wisdom
Of the Gods

There shall be a pause of perhaps five heartbeats. If the Oracle feels inspired of the Crone she may speak more, then replace the mask in its place and return to the coven.

The Priestess and the Priest shall lead the procession in a circuitous route back to the cauldron. The Priest shall then go before the cauldron and, raising high his staff, call:

We give thanks to the God
For knowledge of times to build,
And times to tear down.
Power of will, and strength of soul
Turn life's great wheel
And make us ever better
From life, to life, to life.
Blessed Be!
All: BLESSED BE!

The Priestess shall then go before the cauldron, and raising high her staff, call:

That which we have seen, and heard,
Regard it well.
There are turning points to all things,
Not only of this world, but others,
In the affairs of humankind
And with the Gods themselves.
Thus it is, and shall be
To the ends of the universe
And beyond time.
For this wisdom
We thank the Goddess.
Blessed Be!
All: BLESSED BE!

There shall be a pause of nine heartbeats. Then shall the Priest turn to the coven, rap thrice upon the ground with his staff, and proclaim:

This rite of Midsummer
Is ended.
Merry meet and merry part.
All: MERRY MEET AND MERRY PART.

For those who are so inclined, this would be the time and place to leave the ritual area and spend the rest of the night in a solitary wilderness vigil, considering and meditating upon that which has been said. For all others, this now is a time for festival, for feasting and drink, for dancing and for good company.

ABOUT THE MIDSUMMER RITE

This rite, usually and in most lands a cheery celebration of the bounty of summer, is here an examination
of the deeper aspects of this season, and the nature of
life itself. The ancient Celtic and ancient Grecian
sources are much of the root of this ceremony. The
Maiden, Mother, and Crone, the King of the Declining
Year and the Young King are of the British Isles, while
the profound Mystery content and the use of masks is
drawn from classical and pre-classical Greece.

Harvest
Festivals

utumn is the golden season of harvest . . . of richness and bounty.

Our ancestors, being closer to the land, knew it as the busy, cheerful culmination of the growing season . . . Families were busy with reaping and threshing, and those hired to help with the harvest made the families seem even bigger than before. The whole farm bustled with activity . . . every shed, every grain bin, every storage area was occupied.

Along with the home-grown food gathered in from field and garden, fruits from the orchards and nuts and berries from the forest were brought home. Large amounts of food were preserved for the winter, so that the houses were sweet with the scent from the bubbling pots and jars.

A very busy time, and a rewarding one . . . in the way that only solid physical labor can be rewarding.

When all was done and the harvests laid in, celebration was definitely in order . . . for one more year had passed, and the very-present gamble implicit in gaining sustenance from the earth had once more been won.

THE PAGAN HARVEST FESTIVALS

There are three major Pagan festivals which take place during the Harvest season, and which have come to emphasize different aspects of the seasonal ingathering. These are traditionally placed at "Lammas" — July 31/August 1, Autumn Equinox — generally falls around Sept. 21-23, and "Hallowmas" — Oct. 31/Nov. 1. Note that Pagan holidays always commence on the eve of the festival.

Although all three of these are in the nature of harvest celebrations, through time and tradition, these festivals have taken on very distinctive characteristics, highlighting different aspects of the harvest season. Lammas has come to be the festival which gives special honor to the grain harvest and the mystical symbolism of the grain. Autumn Equinox marks the balance point in the solar year when day and night are equal in length, and is also the traditional "Harvest Home" or Thanksgiving for Pagans, and Hallowmas marks the beginning of winter when all must be gathered in and the herds must be thinned in preparation for the cold season ahead. Hallowmas is also the feast which honors the dead.

We realize, of course, that people living in different climes will be gathering in their crops at different dates, and that some northern areas have very short growing seasons, while very warm and subtropical areas are lucky enough to have a year-round harvest.

Fortunately, the intent of modern Paganism is to bring the individual in tune with the tides of nature, and so individuals must adjust the festivals so that they will be meaningful to life in their own locale. Thus, we present the aforementioned dates, traditional to Pagan systems which have come to us from north-western Europe, as good, general, arbitrary dates to commemorate the seasonal holidays, but each Pagan family should move the feast dates to better suit their locale, if this is necessary, and the rituals can also be altered accordingly.

HARVEST FESTIVALS AROUND THE WORLD

Since harvest festivals have been important to ancient peoples the world over, and continue to be celebrated in many lands, there is a vast body of delightful old customs associated with these. Many of these old traditions have survived in our present-day celebrations, both pagan and secular (as in Thanksgiving), and we've made use of our research into these to enhance our own Neopagan system.

AUTUMN FIRES

In the other gardens
　And all up the vale,
From the autumn bonfires
　See the smoke trail!

Pleasant summer over
　And all the summer flowers,
The red fire blazes,
　The gray smoke towers.

Sing a song of seasons!
　Something bright in all!
Flowers in the summer,
　Fires in the fall!

　　　　　Robert Louis Stevenson

Lammas
Festivals

ammas is a cross-quarter day, falling at 15 degrees Leo, (midway between the Summer Solstice and the Autumn Equinox), although tradition has now attached this holiday to August Eve, July 31/August 1.

"Lammas" marks the beginning of the Harvest Season. The name of this festival is derived from the Anglo-Saxon "Hlaf-mas"—a celebration honoring grain, the main staple of life.

Around the world, the principle staple crop consumed, and therefore honored in harvest festivals, differs from region to region. In England, wheat is preferred; in Scotland and Ireland, oats; in the New World and Australia, maize (Indian Corn) was originally more important to survival but has since been replaced in popularity by wheat; and in the Orient, rice is the staple crop. American Neopagan Lammas celebrations will probably focus primarily on wheat-foods for baking, but all of the aforementioned food-stuffs participate in the same symbolism and can be included.

NOTE: Traditionally, the words "grain", "corn", and "cereal" have been practically interchangeable, generally referring to plants of which the seeds are suitable for food. However, I've chosen to use the word "grain" because many Americans are confused by the other terms. For example, in Europe, the word "corn" is used to refer to a variety of crops, whereas in American popular usage, it is used exclusively to denote maize. Likewise, most Americans use the word "cereal" strictly to denote certain kinds of breakfast foods.

Ancient peoples viewed the grain as a manifestation of the divine force . . . personified as the "green man", a resilient kind of god-figure, growing sturdy and solid through spring and summer, cut down by the Harvest's scythe, sleeping through the cold winter in the bosom of the Mother-Earth, and returning once again, as a reborn infant, clothed in green with the spring. Our ancestors honored this cycle from birth through growth, consummation, sacrifice, death, and inevitable rebirth with rituals, processions, dances, and feasts.

Grain also symbolizes ancestry and forms a link to the past, representing, as it does, the unbroken chain of the consummation of countless generations of life and death. (Perhaps this is why it was a Ukrainian custom to refer to a sheaf of wheat as "the forefather").

Bread and brew—products of the grain harvest— represent the mystery of transformation, the modification of natural food by fire, (boiling, baking, roasting, etc.). This symbolism, the metamorphosis from raw to cooked, can be carried so far as to represent that thing which we call civilization. (Indeed, civilization came into existence as a result of the agricultural arts—the accumulated and refined knowledge of planting, harvesting and storing—in which the cultivation of grains is of central importance).

As an extension of this symbolism, the oven becomes a sacral, life-transforming vessel. Thus, it plays a role in the female mysteries, for it can be compared to the womb, and it comes as no surprise that, (according to folklorist Jakob Grimm), women once performed their devotions before the oven. In some of the ancient mystery cults, the feminine was viewed as the repository of transformation, laying the foundations of human culture, which is transformed nature.

Since many of us no longer live close to nature, and since our supermarkets carry food and grain in year-round supply, we can't fully comprehend how much this staple meant to our ancestors, especially since the supply would become scarcer as the months progressed. We can still appreciate the mystical symbolism of the grain, and so today, our Pagan households celebrate the Lammas holiday with brewing and baking. Several families may gather together on Lammas or the week-end closest to it, and members of both sexes, youngsters and oldsters, participate in a food-making "bee". Several kinds of bread are baked, (making lots extra to carry home to family, friends, and neighbors), and some new batches of wine and ale are also started.

Of course, interspersed with this hard work are recess sessions for fun and games, music and dance.

Lammas Meal

he Lammas supper is the simplest feast in the festival year. The main course is the bread and the brew (beer, wine, ale . . . your choice), which have been consecrated earlier. The purpose is to contemplate the symbolism of the grain . . . the continuity of life, the link between generations past, present and future.

The table is set beforehand with a goblet for each person present, and if desired, a small plate for each person. (Some may prefer a more "back-to-nature" sort of meal, with no plates or utensils). The bread and the drink are set in the center of the table (or circle), and to either side are the white festival candles. The festival area may be decorated with various grains and grain motifs.

The master of the household bids all present to gather 'round the table, saying:

Let us now keep the feast of Lammas!

All are seated, and the master bids them:

Let us now join hands and purify ourselves,
Breathing in the life force of the universe,
And expelling all evil from us.
Now are we prepared to partake of
*   the bread and the brew*
That has been duly consecrated for the
*   Lammas meal.*

The eldest child then takes up the loaf of bread and goes 'round the table (or circle) breaking off bread for all seated there, while the house-mistress says:

Take now of the bread,
And know of the grain of which you partake
As the latest of countless generations—
Growing to fruitfulness,
And in dying, giving of the seeds
From which new life shall spring!

The master says:

Know that every seed, every grain is
*   the record of times most ancient,*
And a promise of all that shall be.
Partake of the bread,
And know of life eternal, and
*   of Immortality!*

The mistress then says:

> *With this knowledge are our souls sustained*
> *In this season of waning light and*
> *   increasing darkness.*

The eldest child, or one so chosen, then takes up the brew and goes around the table (or circle) to fill all the glasses as the master says:

> *Take now of the brew,*
> *And know of the transformation*
> *Of simple fruit and grain into sparkling*
> *   elixir.*
> *As this wine has undergone change,*
> *So by life's cauldron shall we!*

The mistress then says:

> *As this brew gives the enchantment*
> *   of the Divine*
> *Or abasement into lower realms,*
> *So do all humans rise or fall in each life*
> *As their own will and strength determines.*

The master says:

> *Partake of the brew*
> *And know of the cauldron of rebirth*
> *And the power of Will!*

The mistress then replies:

> *As in the bread, and in the brew,*
> *So also it is with us.*
> *The Mysteries of ancient times are with*
> *   us still.*
> *May the wide-ruling Powers and the*
> *   ancestral gods*
> *Lay their blessings upon this meal!*

The master of the household then instructs his family:

> *Let us now complete this Lammas feast,*
> *Ever mindful of the significance it bears!*

The family then proceeds with the simple meal. For the festivities afterward, readings and dramatizations of ancient myths and legends are appropriate.

Harvest Rite

This rite should be held out-of-doors if possible, or if inside, then within a spacious chamber that can be appropriately decorated for the season. All should work together in preparing the place of the festival so that it has the appropriate look and feel of late summer and the fruits of the fields. The ritual area should be decorated, for example, with grain, fruits, maize, vegetables, and nuts, as well as with leaves and flowers.

At the center of the festival place should be placed an image of the Goddess, and a selection of all the grain, fruits, etc., arranged close about the statue. A large and perhaps ornate candle should be placed before the Goddess image and lit before the rite. If such is available, a sickle should be tied with golden ribbons and laid before the image of the Lady; if such is not available, then a knife should be so festooned and placed before the image.

Also before the Goddess image should be placed four earthenware cups: one should contain fresh, cold water, one rich dark loam, one to hold incense that is lit, and one to hold the stub of a burning candle. Many votive candles should be placed near the center of the area, one for each person taking part in the rite and numerous others to be placed about the ritual area. Wine, cakes, and other refreshments should likewise be placed about the image of the Lady. All should costume themselves appropriately.

When all is in readiness each should take a candle and set it before him or her (if outdoors then candles should be placed in glass jars to make then windproof) to be lit later. Other than the lights before the image of the Lady, all shall be dark.

All shall sit in quiet meditation for some minutes, thinking on the ways in which this festival was celebrated by our distant ancestors during ancient pagan times. The one chosen to be the Priest, when he feels the time is appropriate, shall quietly tell all to link hands and perhaps form a circle about the ritual area if the celebrants are sufficient in number. The meditation should continue for yet a longer time. The one chosen to be the Priestess shall, when she feels the time is appropriate, say:

Friends, I now bid you
To strike now the lights which you hold,
For this is a season of bounty, and of joy,
Worthy to be celebrated,

As in times far ancient
Before our Gods
And in their honor.

All do light their candles. The Priest and Priestess light the additional ones and give them to others, to be placed about the edge of the ritual area, saying to each:

Place this light
At the edge of our festival
So that the Old Ones
May be with us.

One within the ceremony should be chosen to give salutations to each quarter, or one person chosen to give the call to the East, one to the South, one to the West, and one to the North. The Watcher of the East shall call:

Far winds, blow clean and clear,
Sweep free through the skies
And be with us here.

The Watcher of the South shall call:

Blessed Sun and lands of warmth,
Give comfort, and brightness, and strength
And be with us here.

The Watcher of the West shall call:

Oceans, lakes, and streams,
Wash clear, and bright, and fresh
And be with us here.

The Watcher of the North shall call:

Mountains, meadows, and forests,
Bring forth life, and richness, and beauty
And be with us here.

Then the Priestess shall say:

We call now upon the blessed Lady,
Queen of the Harvest, giver of life
And of plenty
Since before time began,
Give to us, as of old,
Thy joy, and beauty, and power.

The Priest shall then say:

We call upon the Lord of the Harvest,
Sacred King, giver of riches
And of protection
Since before time began,
Give to us, as of old,
Thy strength, and laughter, and power.

The Priestess then says to all in the rite:

Let us now, as of old,
Make a consecration of the harvest
And mark here the fullness of the season.
For life does fulfill its cycle
And lead to life anew
In the eternal chain of the living
That has stretched and broken
Since time immemorial.

She takes up the sickle (or knife) and an ear of maize still in its husk and leads the procession deosil (clockwise) about the ritual area, with the image of the Goddess at the center, no less than thirteen times. The Priest and others shall beat a rhythm and all shall chant:

THE YEAR WHEEL TURNS
AND BOUNTY COMES

This should be repeated again and again. It is appropriate for members of the group to carry fruits, vegetables, grains, nuts and such in the procession, as well as their candles.

Finally, the Priestess shall stop the procession as she stands before the image of the Goddess. The Priest shall take her light and hold it as she holds up and before her the sickle and the ear of maize calling:

O great and timeless Goddess
We give thanks for this the season
Of the harvest.
We can give nothing that is not
Already thine,
Yet accept, with our love,
This offering and this sacrifice
To thee, O gracious and beautiful one.

She tears the husks from the maize and cuts it in twain

with the sickle, then says to those in the festival:

That the season of plenty
Shall return once more,
And in commemoration of life
Springing ever new from death,
I charge you now to bury
Within the Earth
The offering we have made to Her.

If the rite is outdoors the husks and maize shall be buried on the spot, if indoors they shall be laid before the image of the Lady and buried after the ceremony.

The Priest then says to all present within the area:

This is a time of joy.
Let us now eat, and drink,
And, each within ourselves,
Invite the Gods to be with us here
And to enjoy this time with us.

He opens the wine and pours the first cups as the Priestess hands out the cakes. All shall now eat, drink, sing, dance, and generally enjoy themselves.

When the Priestess and Priest feel that the festival should end they shall call all together to close the rite. The Priest shall say:

Friends this festival now ends.
Let us now give thanks to the Goddess
And to the God
For this time of richness
And for the times of magic
Which shall come.
Watchers, call now
To the far quarters.

The Watcher of the East shall call:

Far winds blow clean and pure,
We give you thanks for being here.

The Watcher of the South shall call:

Blessed Sun and lands of warmth,
We give you tnaks for being here.

The Watcher of the West shall call:

Oceans, lakes, and streams,
We give you thanks for being here.

The Watcher of the North shall call:

Mountains, meadows, and forests,
We give you thanks for being here.

The Priestess shall hold her arms aloft in salute and call:

O Lady of magic and beauty,
O king of strength and power,
Creatures of all wild places
And beings of all far realms . . .
We give you greeting, and love, and farewell.
Blessed Be!
All: BLESSED BE!

And finally the Priest shall say:

Put out the lights about us
For this rite is ended.

ABOUT THE HARVEST RITE

This ceremony is drawn from Central European sources for the words but the thanks to the gods of nature as well as the offering for continued bounty in the years to come are common to all of Europe and the British Isles. It is best followed by feasting, dancing, and singing.

ABOUT THE WINTER RITE

In form, imagery, and content, this ritual is purely Russian! Winter is long and harsh in that vast land, and spring will come late. The God whose aspect is most obvious is the mighty Frost King, cold and powerful. The Goddess as ever may be honored as Maiden, Mother, and Crone, but Her pre-eminent aspect is that of the icy, beautiful Snow Queen. The Divine Child of hope and of the coming year's bounty is born at this season, for from the Winter Solstice the days will gradually be lengthening . . . but for a long time yet one must live out the winter in reflective solitude, meditating on winter's inhospitible beauty, and sharing the company of family and of close friends.

Winter
Rite

his ritual is intended for performance during the middle of the winter, and ideally, near the time of the Full Moon. The altar is placed at the center of the ritual area, facing to the north. On it should be placed an image of the Goddess, draped in fur or white cloth, a representation of the God which most appropriately would be a small statuette of a stag, and symbols of the four elemental kingdoms: the Tarot aces of swords, pentacles, wands, and cups would suffice, though more elaborate symbolism may be used. If an altar cloth is used it should be white in color, with gold and silver trim. Pine scented incense should be lit before the rite and three candles, white, red, and black, placed before the image of the Lady. Small sleigh type bells should be on the altar or before it, for use in calling the quarters during the rite.

The area of the ritual should be decorated with the symbolism of winter: bare branches, evergreen, and that which might suggest snow and ice. Fur may be worn as trim on the robes, cloaks, or other ritual garb worn for this ceremony. Prior to and during the rite there may be soft background music which is suggestive of winter. Thirteen small candles should be place about the outer edge of the ritual circle.

To begin, all shall enter the ritual area and seat themselves about the altar, with the Priestess and Priest sitting together before the altar. At this point there shall be no light, and all shall be dark. All will hold hands and meditate in silence on the cold darkness of winter, of the season for turning inwards, and on the ways in which our distant Pagan ancestors celebrated this season in times long past. Some time should pass.

When she feels that the time is right, the Priestess shall say:

> At this time do we know the dark of the year.
> The season of life is past, and all is cold.
> Emptiness and bleakness are all about.
> Let us now give honor to the Triple Goddess
> That the season may be made better
> Through the birth of the Divine Child,
> The Golden Newborn Solstice Sun.

She strikes a flame, and lights the white candle before the Goddess image, saying:

> White do we light for the Maiden,
> Thou divine and joyous child.
> Fresh and new as the driven snow

Is the taper which is Her symbol.
We give greetings to the Blessed One.

She strikes a flame, and lights the red candle before the Goddess image, saying:

Red do we light for the Mother,
Thou warm embracing Queen of Creation.
Scarlet as the beauty of the winter sunset
Is the taper which is Her symbol.
We give greetings to the Regal One.

She strikes a flame, and lights the black candle before the Goddess image, saying:

Black do we light for the Crone,
Thou keeper of the magical mysteries.
Ebon as the night of sleet
Is the taper which is Her symbol.
We give greetings to the Wise One.

One or more of those within the ritual area, as appointed by the Priestess, shall proceed deosil (clockwise) about the circle, starting and ending at the North, lighting the small candles. As this is done the Priest says:

As the light grows about us,
So also may the presence
Of the Old Gods,
Who come forth now in triumph,
Glow where we now stand.
May magic and mystery and beauty
Be with us now
In this, the Season of the White Goddess,
And the divine Child of Light.
So mote it be!
All: SO MOTE IT BE!

The Priestess goes to the East, and holds out her arms in greeting. Small bells are jingled and she summons:

All hail to thee, skies of wind and of storm.
Blow ye clear, cold, and sharp
Over the sleeping land.
Cast thy spell, O Great Ones,
And remain.
Blessed Be!
All: BLESSED BE!

The Priest goes to the South, and holds out his arms in

greeting. Small bells are jingled and he summons:

> *All hail to thee, far desert lands and*
> *and places warm,*
> *Return ye soon, and with bounty,*
> *To bring back the warm seasons.*
> *Cast thy spell, O Great Ones,*
> *And remain,*
> *Blessed Be!*

All: BLESSED BE!

The Priestess goes to the West, and holds out her arms in greeting. Small bells are jingled and she summons:

> *All hail to thee, crystalline lakes and*
> *rimed streams.*
> *Frozen in glittering beauty.*
> *Be ye places of mystery, and portals elvish.*
> *Cast thy spell, O Great Ones,*
> *And remain.*
> *Blessed Be!*

All: BLESSED BE!

The Priest goes to the North, and holds out his arms in greeting. Small bells are jingled and he summons:

> *All hail to thee, endless realms of snow,*
> *Frozen tundra, forests in white, and*
> *mountains sheathed in ice.*
> *Rest deeply in glistening silence and mystery.*
> *Cast thy spell, O Great Ones,*
> *And remain.*
> *Blessed Be!*

All: BLESSED BE!

The Priestess and Priest stand before the altar, facing North. There is a pause of five heartbeats and the bells are jingled twice. The Priest evokes:

> *O Hearty God of Frost*
> *Whose beard is of shining ice*
> *And whose staff turns all to crystal,*
> *Thou whose Art is not of these worlds,*
> *Be with us, we do ask.*
> *Give us of thy sharp joy.*
> *Let us hear the crackling of thy laughter,*
> *And may we know better*
> *Of thy wisdom and thy magic.*
> *Blessed Be!*

All: BLESSED BE!

There is a pause of five heartbeats and the bells are jingled thrice. The Priestess evokes:

> *O most regal Queen of Snow*
> *Whose glistening jewels glitter about us,*
> *And whose sorceries turn all to sparkling*
>   *white.*
> *Shining empress whose crown is of the arctic*
>   *stars*
> *And whose mantle is the icy fire of the*
>   *borealis,*
> *Be with us, we do ask.*
> *May we know thy cold and distant beauty,*
> *And may we know better*
> *Of thy wisdom and thy magic.*
> *Blessed Be!*

All: BLESSED BE!

The incense is renewed, and there is a pause of at least thirteen heartbeats. Four within the ritual area shall earlier have been appointed by the Priestess and Priest to give the Response of the Four Quarters. They shall at this time take their respective positions. (If the group of Pagans is small, these roles may be taken by the Priestess and the Priest.)

The Priestess raps thrice upon the altar and says:

> *In this the Season of the White Goddess*
> *And the time of the Divine Child,*
> *What wisdom says the Watcher of the East?*

East:

> *This is a time for entering wilderness,*
> *And seeking its magical strengths.*
> *A time for standing alone and godlike,*
> *And seeing all things clearly.*
> *It is a season of Joy!*

There shall be a silence of perhaps the space of 30 heartbeats. The Priest raps thrice upon the altar and says:

> *In this, the Season of the White Goddess*
> *And the time of the Divine Child,*
> *What wisdom says the Watcher of the South?*

South:

> *This is a time of active seeking,*
> *Both without in Nature and within oneself.*

*Eagerness and resolution shall concern
    mysteries,
And create results.
It is a season of Courage!*

There shall be a silence perhaps the space of 30 heart-beats. The Priestess raps thrice upon the altar and says:

*In this, the Season of the White Goddess
And the time of the Divine Child,
What wisdom says the Watcher of the West?*

West:

*This is a time for devotion to the Way of the
    Wild Places
And seeking the calmness of solitary locales.
A time for finding understanding,
And confiding only in trusted friends.
It is a season of Meditation!*

There shall be a silence perhaps the space of 30 heart-beats. The Priest raps thrice upon the altar and says:

*In this, the Season of the White Goddess
And the time of the Divine Child,
What wisdom says the Watcher of the North?*

North:

*This is a time to know the endurance of the
    hills,
And to so grow in one's own inner firm-
    ness
A time for scrupulousness and thorough-
    ness
And considering all things.
It is a season of Confidence!*

There shall be a silence perhaps the space of 30 heart-beats. At this time other additions may be made to the rite, such as a circle dance, a procession, or music as desired by the ones in the rite and with the guidance of the Priestess and the Priest. When this has been accomplished the ceremony shall be closed. The Priestess shall go to the East, and hold out her arm in salute. Small bells are jingled and she says:

*We thank thee, skies of wind and of storm,
And give our blessings to thy far realms.*

> *Blessed Be!*
All: BLESSED BE!

The Priestess shall go to the West, and hold out her arm in salute. Small bells are jingled and she says:

> *We thank thee, crystalline lakes and rimed
>   streams.*
> *And give our blessings to thy far realms.*
> *Blessed Be!*
All: BLESSED BE!

The Priest shall go to the North, and hold out his arm in salute. Small bells are jingled and he says:

> *We thank thee, endless lands of snow,*
> *And give our blessings to thy far realms.*
> *Blessed Be!*
All: BLESSED BE!

The Priestess and Priest stand before the altar, facing North. There is a pause of five heartbeats and the bells are jingled twice. The Priest says:

> *O joyous God of Frost*
> *We thank thee for thy bright presence*
>   *here.*
> *We have been honored to have your spirit*
> *Here among us.*
> *Farewell, and blessed be!*
All: FAREWELL, AND BLESSED BE!

There is a pause of five heartbeats and the bells are jingled thrice. The Priestess says:

> *O magnificent Queen of Snow*
> *We thank thee for thy crystal presence here.*
> *We have been honored to have your spirit*
> *Here among us.*
> *Farewell, and blessed be!*
All: FAREWELL, AND BLESSED BE!

She puts out the candles before the Goddess image and says:

> *The Goddess, the God, and the Child*
> *Have been honored.*
> *This rite of Winter is done.*
> *Merry meet and merry part.*

The Meanings of Flowers

Rose Acacia . . . . Friendship
Amaryllis . . . . Beautiful but Timid
Blue Bell . . . . Constancy
Buttercup . . . . Riches; Memories of Childhood
Camellia . . . . Gratitude, Perfect Loveliness
Carnation . . . . Pure and Deep Love
White Clover . . . . I Promise
Four Leaved Clover . . . . Be Mine
Red Columbine . . . . Anxious and trembling
Dahlia . . . . Dignity and elegance
Daffodil . . . . Unrequited love
Garden Daisy . . . . I share your feelings
Single Field Daisy . . . . I will think of it
Dandelion . . . . Oracle; Coquetry
Foxglove . . . . Insincerity; Occupation
Rose Geranium . . . . I prefer you
Honeysuckle . . . . Devoted love; Fidelity
Hyacinth . . . . Constancy; Benevolence
White Jasmine . . . . Amiability
Jonquil . . . . Desire; Affection returned
Lavender . . . . Mistrust
Purple Lilac . . . . First Emotions of love
White Lily . . . . Majesty; Purity
Lily of the Valley . . . . Return of Happiness
Lupine . . . . Dejection
Magnolia . . . . Love of Nature
Marigold . . . . Sacred Affection
Garden Marigold . . . . Grief; Chagrin
Mignonette . . . . Your qualities surpass your charms
Morning Glory . . . . Coquetry; Affection
Myrtle . . . . Love in Absence
Purple Pansy . . . . You occupy my thoughts
Periwinkle . . . . Sweet Memories
Phlox . . . . Our hearts are united
Pimpernel . . . . Rendezvous; Change
Primrose . . . . Modest worth; Silent love
Rhododendron . . . . Agitation
Rosebud . . . . Confession of Love
Red Rose . . . . I love you
White Rose . . . . Silence
Yellow Rose . . . . Infidelity, Unfaithfulness
Snapdragon . . . . Presumption
Snowball . . . . Goodness; Thoughts of Heaven
Snowdrop . . . . Consolation; A friend in adversity
Sunflower . . . . False Riches
Sweet Pea . . . . A meeting
Red Tulip . . . . Declaration of love
Blue Violet . . . . Faithfulness
White Violet . . . . Purity; Candor; Modesty
Zinnia . . . . I mourn your absence

Supplemental
Rites

Calling Down the Moon

his rite is a revised version of the old Outer Court Calling Down the Moon. This new ritual is highly eclectic, drawing material from many sources including the traditional charge of the Goddess, material used by Amtrad groups, from the *Transformations of Lucius* by Apelius, from Leland's *Aradia*, and many others. The *Outer Court Book of Shadows*, originally devised by Ed Fitch, has been around for a long time now and passed through many hands. This rite is a sample of the Outer Court rituals, currently under revision.

THE RITUAL

The circle is cast in the usual or preferred manner. Additional incense is put into the brazier. All join hands in meditation as the Priestess, standing in the north says:

> *As we breathe deeply in and out.*
> *It is not just air we take in . . .*
> *It is the soft silver light of the Moon,*
> *Symbol of our Lady.*
> *With every pore in our bodies*
> *So we breathe in and out.*
> *And so does this circle become a fitting place*
> *For our Lady's presence.*

The Priest, standing to the south of the altar, and across from the Priestess, raises his arms, saying:

> *We are the children of the Moon.*
> *We are born of shining light.*
> *When the Moon shoots forth a ray*
> *We see within it the Goddess . . .*
> *   and ourselves.*

The Priestess addresses all in the circle:

> *What we call in our hearts*
> *Goes forth everywhere . . .*
> *   echoing*
> *Beyond the stars themselves.*
> *And we need have no doubt*
> *That we are heard.*

Then all raise their arms (in the Egyptian supplicant position) as the Priest calls on the ancient names. The Priestess stands in the pentagram position.

Priest: Hearken unto our call, Diana!
   Lady of the Silver Bowl
All: IO EVOHE Diana!
Priest: Hearken unto our call, Aradia!
   Beloved Daughter of the Sun and Moon
All: IO EVOHE Aradia!
Priest: Hearken unto our call Queen Isis!
   Eternal Queen of the Immortals
All: IO EVOHE Isis!
Priest: Hearken unto our call Arianrhod!
   Lady of the Silver Wheel
All: IO EVOHE Arianrhod!
Priest: Hearken unto our call Huldana!
   Queen of the Night faring Beings
All: IO EVOHE Huldana!

After the salute the Priest motions for all to kneel, facing the Priestess: She feels herself at one with the Goddess as she holds out her arms in the Goddess (Isis) position as she gives the charge:

> *I am the Star that rises from the dark*
>   *and twilight Sea.*
> *Bringer of dreams, ruler of destiny.*
> *Though I am known by a thousand*
>   *thousand names,*
> *Yet the whole round Earth doth*
>   *venerate Me.*
> *I am Nature and the beauty of the*
>   *Green Earth.*
> *Mistress of all the elements.*
> *Sovereign of all things spiritual,*
> *Queen of Heaven, Queen of Hell,*
> *Queen of the dead*
> *Queen of the blessed immortals.*
> *The Single Manifestation of all Gods and*
>   *Goddesses that Are.*
> *Hearken unto My Words and look at Me!*
> *Forget not whence thou didst come*
>   *and to where thou art called!*
> *And in the fulfillment of Time*
> *Thou shalt KNOW*
> *That I am that which is WITH thee, and*
>   *IN thee, and OF thee!*
> *And thus shall thy Spirit attain*
> *To the deepest Mystery of Life.*
> *And thus shall thine Inmost Divine Self be*
>   *enfolded in the ecstasies of the Infinite!*

These things have I made Law,
Enduring for the million million ages.

The Priestess pauses. She should feel that she is a vessel for the Lady, and that the Goddess speaks and acts through her. At this point she may speak further, if the Goddess within her desires so. When she is done, she will lower her arms and the Priest shall say:

O lovely Goddess of the Moon,
Fairer far than any star,
Gracious Lady, our thanks to Thee,
For coming to us from afar!

He motions for the rest of the coven to sit, and says to the Priestess:

Will My Lady join us?

The coven then proceeds with Cakes and Wine, and then the closing of the circle.

Goddess (Isis) Position

MAGICAL SAYINGS

To keep a cat or dog from running away, chase it three times around the hearth, and rub it against the chimney shaft.

When the crickets sing in the house, things go luckily.

When you've bought a cat, bring it in with its head facing the street and not the house; else it will not stay.

from Grimm's Teutonic Mythology

If a bee alights upon your head and stays there you will be a great person in after years.

It is luck to take a horse through your house.

When you have a new coat do not put it on empty, but put something into the pocket for luck.

When rosemary grows in the garden, the mistress rules the house.

To put on any article of clothing accidentally inside out is regarded by some as an omen of luck; but it is necessary to wear the reversed portion of attire wrong side out till the usual time comes to take it off if one wishes the luck to hold, otherwise the good fortune is immediately lost.

If the bees swarm high upon the trees, it is regarded as an omen that the price of grain will be high, but should they swarm low, the value is likely to be less.

Should a child be born with its hand open it is believed to indicate that it will be of a bountiful disposition in the future.

A bird falling down a chimney is a bearer of good luck, and if a bee flies into a room it is thought to be a harbinger of good news.

In some places it is customary to always place a bed parallel with the boards in the floor, as it is thought unlucky to sleep crossing them.

Country folk in Suffolk say, if a broom is left accidentally in the corner of a room after it has been swept, it is a sign that strangers will visit the house during the day.

(From Folktales and Superstitions of York, Lincoln, Derby, 7 Nottingham—1895)

Ceremony of Cakes and Wine

 hen a Craft ritual is held and a great circle is cast, there is traditionally a pause for refreshment within the circle when consecrated food and drink are served. This ceremony is usually referred to as "cakes and wine" or "cakes and ale." This is a time for group members to relax and engage in meaningful discussion of magical subjects.

The following simple blessings for Outer Court use are based on and inspired by the Aradia lore, and can be used in consecrating the cakes and wine which are ritually eaten in the circle:

THE BLESSING OF MEAL, OR CAKES

This blessing can be performed while preparing and baking the cakes, or it can be performed as part of the ritual over already prepared cakes. An alternate way of doing this would be to do the first part of the conjuration during preparation, and the second part during the rite.

A popular way of serving ritual cakes is to use crescent or pentacle shaped cookies. Recipes are best which include milk, eggs, and honey in the ingredients.

The Priestess holds her hand over the dough mixture or over the cakes in an attitude of blessing, (in the case of already prepared cakes or cookies, she does this as they lie on the vessel held forward by the Priest). She visualizes them being imbued with energy as she says:

> *I conjure thee, O Meal!*
> *Who art indeed our body since without thee*
> *We could not live, thou who — at first as seed —*
> *Before becoming flower went in the earth*
>
> *Where all deep secrets hid, and then when flour ground*
> *Didst dance like dust in the wind, and yet meanwhile*
> *Didst bear with thee in flitting, secrets strange!*
>
> *I conjure thee, O meal!*
> *That as we take part of thee*
> *We take part of the wisdom of the Ancients,*
> *We learn more of the fields and the*

forests,
We see the ancient Way,
And understand the ancient lore.

The Priestess then serves one cake to each member of the circle, who upon receiving it, breaks off a small piece which is set upon the offering dish. (These small offerings are later set outside and left for the wild animals). Each member of the circle should acknowledge the food with a small bow or courtesy to the Priestess.

THE BLESSING OF WINE

The communal cup (a special chalice reserved for ritual purposes) is poured full of wine. The Priest holds up the chalice and the Priestess places her hand over it in an attitude of blessing, saying:

I conjure thee, O wine!
Thou who at first didst grow from
nothing
By light of sun and light of moon.
The swelling, ripened grape
The blood of the earth pressed soon!

I conjure thee, O wine!
That as we drink of thee
We drink of the power of the gods,
Of fire, and lightning, and rain,
Of things that are wild and free!

The Priestess then goes about the circle and offers the chalice to each member in turn, who takes a sip thereof, acknowledging the drink with a bow. The chalice is then set back upon the altar, and the drink which remains in the chalice is later poured out upon the ground, usually before a special tree, as a libation.

After this basic sacramental rite, the Priest may then pour out wine or beverage in individual goblets for those present in the circle, who may then relax and converse over the beverage.

LIBATIONS

It is proper, when one is partaking of food and drink outdoors, and particularly in the mountains, the forests, along a lake or seashore, to make a libation to the Goddess in Her aspect as Earth Mother. Either before or after eating, whichever seems more appropriate to you or is more practical, go off to a growing tree or

bush and drop a few crumbs of food at its base, and pour out nearby a few drops of drink. Then, say the following aloud to yourself:

Hail Earth, Mother of all!
May your fields increase and flourish,
Your forests grow and spread,
And your waters run pure and free!
Accept my offering, O Earth Mother!
Bring forth that which is good, and
*   sustaining,*
*   For every living thing!*

In France, a number of new calendars were introduced at the time of the Revolution. One of these was a sytem based on nature, devised by the poet Fabre d'Eglantine, who renamed the months and days for the climate of northern France. This calendar was in use until 1806 when Bonaparte restored the Gregorian calendar.

Vendemiaire . . . .vintage   (Sept 22-Oct 21, Libra)
Brumaire . . . . .foggy   (Oct 22-Nov 20, Scorpio)
Frimaire . . . . . . .sleety   (Nov 21-Dec 20, Sagittarius)
Nivose . . . . .snowy   (Dec 21-Jan 19, Capricorn)
Pluviose. . . . . rainy   (Jan 20-Feb 18, Aquarius)
Ventose. . . . . . . windy   (Feb 19-Mar 20, Pisces)
Germinal . . . . . .budding   (Mar 21-Apr 19, Aries)
Floréal. . . . . . . flowery   (Apr 20-May 19, Taurus)
Prairial. . . . . . . pasture   (May 20-June 18, Gemini)
Mesidor . . . . . . .harvest   (June 19-July 18, Cancer)
Thermidor. . . . . . .heat   (July 19-Aug 17, Leo)
Fructidore. . . . . . .fruit   (Aug 18-Sept 16, Virgo)

Feast of the Full Moon

his rite is to be performed at or near the time of the Full Moon, and celebrates the magical waxing and creation aspect of all things. The mood of the entire Feast shall be one of elvish magic, of mystery, of sensuousness, of joy and of power. Ceremonial dress for the evening shall be light, imaginative, dramatic, and in all ways suited to the event.

Prior to the ceremony the place of the feast and ritual shall be fully prepared such that all the events of the evening shall flow smoothly and without interruption.

As the members of the coven arrive, sweet incense shall have been lit, and numerous candles of light pastel colors shall burn about the area. Background music may be medieval music, cheery folk songs, or such as Gwydion's *"Lord of the Dance"* or *"Spring Strathsby."*

Dance, both formal and improvised, shall start the evening. Singing too shall be encouraged. When all have arrived, artificial lights shall be extinquished and all shall proceed out-of-doors where the High Priestess, and/or any other designated for the evening, shall perform a dance in the moonlight to begin building power. The dance shall be magical and sensuous. The music should be faint and, if possible, have a particularly elvish quality to it.

When the dance has been completed all shall adjourn within to begin the readings and meditations. *"She Walks in Beauty"* by Byron, *"My Love Has Wings"* by Wayne, *"Kubla Khan"* by Coleridge, *"High Flight,"* *"Who Rides the Wind,"* *"Helen"* by Poe, Tolkien's *"The Road Goes Ever On,"* *"Elbereth, Gilthoniel,"* *"Goldberry,"* *"Lorien,"* or such. Perhaps two or three minutes should pass between each reading, in order that the text and the implicit meanings may be absorbed by the listeners and the readers.

The art of spinning, as done in the old style with distaff and spindle, should be described. If there is one present who can perform the ancient art, she should demonstrate it. The ancient legends of spinning and of magical spinners should be discussed. Illustrations should be shown of classical and pre-classical Goddess statues shown in attitudes of spinning, and the magical and metaphysical importance of spinning non-being into being, of all things traveling in circles, of creation thus accomplished. Finally a copy of the Pompeiian fresco shall be shown which depicts the Goddess, Her consort, and Her child borne aloft on magical birds which She spins from the distaff which She holds to the Moon, of Her garment and even the sea itself so created. There shall be a period of silence for meditation on the significance of this mystery from ancient times.

There shall be a procession to the temple or other place of the rite, where all shall be seated on cushions. Background music shall be of nightingales, crickets, bob-white, whippoorwill, and other pleasant night sounds. The Invocation and ceremonial Response shall be conducted, to be followed by the inner-plane working, *"Visit to the Cave of Aphrodite,"* after which shall be the Feast of the Full Moon.

When the rite and the feast have been completed, all may relax and socialize.

THE INVOCATION AND RESPONSE OF THE FULL MOON

(The following sections are to be read alternately by the High Priestess and the High Priest).

"This is the time of the fullness of the symbol of our Lady, the Moon. All things wax and wane, and on this evening the powers of life, of magic, and of creation are at their highest. This is the time of building, of doing. It is a time when the veil between the mundane world and the strange and beautiful realms of elphame becomes thin indeed. On this night may one transcend the boundaries of the worlds with ease, and know beauty and enchantment."

"There is a magnificence to this time. The ancients knew well of the mysteries of this night, and used them well to build and to strengthen themselves . . . and to partake of elvish adventures of which we can have but little inkling. Sensuous, mysterious, magical . . . beauty in human form, in dramatic costume, in solid, soaring architecture, the lithe suppleness of our animal brethren, the arrogant magnificence of a spectacular landscape. And more . . . much more . . . "

This is a time for weaving of the inchoate into being, of spinning the strands of space and of time to bring forth Creation. For all does rotate, and turn about upon itself; this is a fundamental principle of the Universe, and a Mystery of the greatest magnitude. The Gods know of it, and we shall also. Weave a spell of moonlight, and fashion with it a fabric of pure magical substance."

"There is a challenge and a joy to building, and creating. The joyous strife of a just battle, of the cascading passion of lovemaking, and even to the birth-pangs in creating a new life. There is the Peace of Aphrodite that follows such as these . . . a thoroughly fulfilling quietude. And it is easy, really. Very easy and

the most natural of things.''

> *"This is a time of traveling unseen in the full moon-light, a time for hearing of elfin music not made by humankind. It is a time for oneness with the forest, with the mountains, with the eternal and life-giving sea, with the warm rains and the bolt of lightning that creates the very spark of life. It is a time for a pilgrimage to the Holy of Holies, to stand at last before the Cauldron of our Lady and to see form, and substance, and being created anew once more.''*

(There shall at this time be a pause. If a deep-throated bell is available, it should be struck once.)

Repeat thou after us:
> *All hail, O Goddess of the silver-rimmed*
> *cauldron!*
> *All hail, thou from whom all does come.*
> *On this night do we give salutation*
> *To the magic of creation*
> *And to the ecstasy of the Gods!*

Incense is added, and a bell is struck.
> *O gracious and beautiful Goddess,*
> *Teach us to weave magic!*
> *Show us thy ancient Art to bring forth*
> *From chaos and from nothingness*
> *That which is Being itself!*
> *Teach us to draw from the Moon,*
> *To spin and to fashion*
> *Fabric magical and pure;*
> *Insubstantial as dew, yet*
> *With the strength of iron.*

A flute is played in a minor key.
> *O most excellent Lady,*
> *Teach us of love, and of beauty,*
> *and of sensuousness.*
> *Teach us of daring, and of adventure.*
> *Show us of the building of spells*
> *Of the spinning and shaping of*
> *moonlight.*
> *Lead our feet in the magical dances*
> *of Power.*
> *Show to us the Paths between the*
> *worlds,*
> *To realms strange, and beautiful.*
> *Lead us through mist and moonlight*

> To places of crystalline rainbow
>   light.
> Groves of enchantment, thy hollow
>   hills of magic,
> And pools and lakes of mystery.

The bell is struck.

> Teach to us, O Lady of Radiance
> To speak the language of the wilds,
> To fly with the freedom of the bird,
> To live the power and grace of the
>   feline,
> To know the ease, the beautiful ease
> Of Creating.
> And to know ecstasy and joy
> To stir the very heights of our being.
>   Blessed Be!

VISIT TO THE CAVE OF APHRODITE

(All shall seat themselves on cushions in comfortable positions near a large mirror, preferably one used for magical purposes. There shall be a pause to allow all to become quiet and serene within themselves, and then shall the narration begin based upon and expanding on the following.)

"It is night, and the moon is full. We stand up where we are, and step out of our bodies, leaving them resting comfortably behind. We go to the mirror and look through; we can see through to the other side and make out a moonlit grassy hill beyond, rising before us. We step through and find ourselves in a warm, moonlit night with a path stretching off to the right across the broad, grassy meadow. We look back briefly and see the portal of our mirror, with the candle lights on the other side; it will be here open and waiting for us when we return. We start up the path in the bright, full moonlight . . .

Forest-covered hills ahead. Bright sky, yet with many bright stars. Smell of evergreen, sound of wind in the tall grass. Some low-lying mist off to one side and the other. We are going up a wide, grassy meadow, with forest well off to one side and the other. Some trees (probably fruit trees) scattered about in the center of the meadow, among which we walk. Wet, soft dew underfoot. Our robes drift in the soft breeze and the moonlight. Gradual upward incline. Sound of night birds, crickets. We move tirelessly up the slight incline, seeming to barely touch the ground. Fireflies flickering here and there in the distance. We go from moonlight to shadow to moonlight among the scattered trees; our tread is al-

most entirely soundless, but we hear the sound of the soft breeze in the tall grass. We look down at our shadows and see that the moon has cast a glistening halo, almost a rainbow in the dew about them.

We glance back and see that we have been going rather rapidly up the hillside. Far behind we can see the rolling hills and on the horizon there seems to be the flickering of a very distant thunderstorm. Far clouds, clear-night otherwise, bright moonlight over the vista. Mist drifting in patches on the meadow. We pass through it, and through the dew. There is the perfume of flowers, the smell of trees and grass. Sounds of small animals in the grass near us. We move quickly, silently, our robes floating in the bright moonlight, our passing through the trees is almost like the passage of moonbeams. Fireflies, far and near. Mist. Haloes about our shadows. Almost as though there may be the shadows of others moving along with us . . . but we can't make them out clearly. Hillside steeper, forest in closer on either side. Ahead the meadow seems to end at a cliff face. Dew. Mist. Auras. Scent of flowers. Sounds of night creatures. We can make out what seems to be the entrance of a cave, with a soft, multicolored glow within.

As we approach closely we see what seem to be glistening minerals encrusting the rock face around the entrance to the cave. We hear what sounds like soft, soft music from within. Rainbow colors inside. Colored mists. We step inside.

We seem to be wrapped in soft light and mists. We notice the odor of the sweetness of flowers. Ahead is a crystal-pure pool of water, catching all colors. Shimmering rainbow mists rise from it. We see a path to the right and follow it next to the pool. There are pools off to the other side as well, in small chambers. The reflections are as though mirrors to other worlds and other times. Sound of soft, soft music. Jewel-like minerals everywhere. Path leads upward, where we see a great cauldron. Mist rising from within, silver heads on edges. Sound of soft, musical whispering. Scent of flowers. We hold up our hands before the cauldron, and we see fine sparkles of light thrown off from our fingers. We weave a pattern with our hands and see, for a moment, a pattern of light in our creation take form, then dissipate to be reality elsewhere. Mists begin to rise from the cauldron. We step up to it, and peer down deep inside to see images of ourselves, as though gazing into a mirror. In these images we begin to see ourselves looking better, more perfect, comelier with fiery glowing auras . . .

images of ourselves looking better in every possible way
. . . within and without! We step back as we throw a kiss
toward the cauldron, as sparkles of light explode in the
air. We look, listen, and then we turn around and begin
to retrace our steps.

Jewel-like minerals. Rainbow mists. Small pools off
to one side in small chambers, seeming to reflect elsewhere and elsewhen. Music, very soft. Crystal-pure pool
of water; rainbow mists; shimmering. Jewelled minerals.
Cave exit. We step outside. Glistening minerals.

Bright moon overhead. Forests to either side. Hillsides. Cliff behind us. Meadow slanting downward before
us. Scattered trees. Grass, dew, drifting mist. Fireflies.
We start down the faint path, our robes floating almost
insubstantial in the moonlight. Auras around our shadows. Wet dew. Fireflies. Sounds of night creatures. We
move rapidly, silently. Far off on the horizon we see
the glow of distant lightning. A storm somewhere. Small
creatures nearby in the grass. Shadows among us, though
we can't make out the figures clearly. Moonlight and
shadow and moonlight as we move rapidly down through
the trees across the meadow. Mist.

Trees farther off to either side now. Fireflies.
Sound of gentle breeze in the grass. Night birds, crickets.
We go down the incline and see the light of our mirror
portal ahead. We go rapidly down the path towards it.
Stop for a moment and look at the forested hillsides,
the mist, the fireflies. Then we step through. We are in
the temple again. We go over to our bodies and settle
comfortably down within them. We are back.

THE FEAST

After a suitable pause for meditation the food shall
be served. Time shall be allowed for most of each speci-
fied food to be consumed while meditating on its significance.

The Priestess and the Priest shall hold their hands
out in an attitude of blessing, as the Priestess says:

O Goddess of beauty, and of magnificence,
O God of laughter and joyous strength.
Cast now Thy blessings on this feast of
 sacrament
That we may honor Thee, and learn of
 Thy mysteries
Of life, of magic of Creating.
Blessed Be!

The Priest says:

> *Eat now of thy vegetables before you.*
> *Salad of the bounty which our Earth*
> *Has created for us.*
> *Ever new, ever fresh, ever excellent.*
> *Know well that the power of life to*
> *   come forth*
> *Is beyond bounds in time and space.*

The Priestess says:

> *Eat now of the bread before you.*
> *Of the grain that forms a link with the*
> *Most Ancient of living things*
> *And with grain that shall sprout and*
> *   grow*
> *For countless eons to come.*
> *Know well that to abide, life must*
> *Draw vitality and power from the*
> *   Earth.*
> *Eat, and know of creation enduring.*

The Priest says:

> *Drink now of the milk before you.*
> *As white as is the moonlight,*
> *Symbol of the Goddess' nourish-*
> *   ment of us.*
> *The first food of all young creatures,*
> *This drawn from the gentle kine.*
> *Know well that all new things,*
> *Created by magic and by mystery,*
> *Must be carefully nurtured, and have*
> *   much care.*
> *Drink, and know the need of love.*

The Priestess says:

> *Eat now of the fruit before you.*
> *The delicate and sweet offering of*
> *   tree and vine.*
> *Of this world, yet transcending it,*
> *For the memory of pleasure long*
> *   remains sweet.*
> *Know well that the finest and lightest of*
> *   nourishment*
> *For the most perfect self*
> *May extend the lives of our souls*
> *Beyond all reckoning.*
> *Eat, and know of immortality.*

The Priest says:

> *Eat now of the egg before you.*
> *Symbol of all that which creation*
>   *may give.*
> *Know of the endless potential of*
> *That which is now, The perfection*
> *Of form and of being*
> *Which is the same from the atom*
> *To the vast wheel of the universe.*
> *Eat, and know of the Beginning.*

The Priestess says:

> *Drink now of the sweet wine before*
>   *you,*
> *Symbol of the light and beautiful magic*
> *Which open portals to the realms of*
>   *strangeness*
> *And of enchantment.*
> *Know that music, and the lure of the*
>   *mysterious*
> *Is the sweetness and most intoxicating*
> *Of all human experience.*
> *Drink, and know of elvish magic.*

The Priest says:

> *Eat now of the light, sweet cake*
>   *before you,*
> *As delicate and as insubstantial as*
> *The fabric of the moonlight.*
> *Yet giving of pleasure, and of*
>   *nourishment.*
> *Know well that magic, and the*
> *Art of creation*
> *Are pleasing to the Gods and to*
>   *humankind.*
> *Eat and know the joy of weaving*
>   *substance.*

The Priestess then says:

> *I bid you now, finish that which ye*
>   *have,*
> *And meditate upon the significance of*
> *That which has been said.*

All shall complete their portions in silence, then shall the rest of the food be served out, and all eat and drink their fill. Discussion and consideration of the ritual and of its meanings is usually the order of the night. Afterwards, the portions set aside as offerings are taken out and left for the wild creatures.

WEATHER LORE

When the cat washes her face over her ears, we shall have a great store of rain.

When cats sit with their tails to the fire or wash their paws behind their ears it betokens a change of weather.

In the Midlands it is believed that if the fire burns brightly after it has been stirred, it is a sign that an absent husband, wife or lover is in good spirits, or if it burns with a pale flame it is an indication of bad weather. When the coals burn with a buzzing sound it signifies that storms are at hand, while a very bright fire is said to be a sign of rain.

*(from The Hand of Destiny—The Folklore
and Superstitions of Everyday Life
C.J.S.Thompson, Singing Tree Press, 1970)*

The last Friday of each month is the almanac index for the next month. If the weather is fair, the month will be likewise; if foul, so will the month be.

Blow out a candle and if the wick continues long to smoulder, look for bad weather. If it goes out quickly, the weather will be fair.

When you hear the first frogs in the spring, you may know the frost is out of the ground.

Rub a cat's back the wrong way, and if you see sparks, it is a sign of cold weather.

When the smoke from a chimney does not rise, but falls to the ground, it is going to storm.

When the squirrels lay in a big store of nuts, look for a hard winter.

When the cattle lie down as soon as they are turned out to pasture in the morning, it is because they feel a rheumatic weariness in their bones, and you can look for a rain soon.

All signs fail in a dry time.

When the farm animals are unusually frisky, it is a sign that it is going to rain.

If you see an old cat running and playing and feeling good, it is a sign the wind is going to blow.

*(from What They Say In New England,
and Other American Folklore
by Clifton Johnson)*

Power
Rituals

Storm Magic

he time at which a thunderstorm is approaching, and when it is in progress, is most meet for the working of magic, for the power of the storm may be called forth to greatly increase the energy directed toward the intended object. At such time as the storm approaches, pick a suitable place for performance of the rite. Ideally it should be out of doors, though some place inside with a very good view of the tempest would also suffice.

This rite is most effective at night, though it may be performed well during the day. The storm is of prime importance: it must be a powerful one.

When a storm comes, go to the middle of a large open place (**exercising caution for lightning**).*
The magic worker can simply stand in the center of the ritual area, making the basic invocations, or ritual implements can be used with an improvised alter of the four elements set in the center. (If an altar is used, each elemental symbol must be placed according to its proper direction, with proper and appropriate symbols used. The symbols should be sturdy enough to withstand the storm. A symbol of the Goddess may be placed at the middle of the altar).

With sword, wand, or athame, depending upon which you prefer to work with, scribe about you a circle about nine feet in diameter, walking sunwise, and perform a brief casting of the circle through the summoning the elements, with sword, wand, or athame held in salute, saying:

To the east, in these or similar words:
> *O winds of storm, I do call thee forth,*
> *Cast thy blessing, I do ask,*
> *Upon the magic which shall be worked*
> *here!*
> (Invoking Pentagram)

To the south, in these or similar words:
> *O fire of lightning, I do call thee*
> *forth,*
> *Bringer of storms and power of*
> *magic,*
> *Aid, I do ask, this powerful spell*
> *Which shall be worked here!*
> (Invoking Pentagram)

To the west, in these or similar words:
> *O torrents of rain, I do call thee forth.*

> *Join me, I do ask, in performing this*
> *Most powerful of magics!*
> (Invoking Pentagram)

To the north, in these or similar words:
> *O earth most heavy and damp, I*
> *do call thee forth,*
> *That I may feel the earth itself move*
> *In the roar of the storm which doth*
> *come*
> *And thou shalt aid in this powerful rite!*
> (Invoking Pentagram)

Invoke the god-force, spreading wide your arms and calling into the wind:
> *Strong and powerful Lord of the Wilds,*
> *Thou who does wield the thunder,*
> *Be with me, I do ask!*
> *And may it be with your steady hand*
> *That I do work here these great magics!*

In like manner, invoke the Goddess-force:
> *Great and magical Lady of the Night*
> *and of the Storm*
> *Thou who doth ride through the thunder*
> *and the tempest*
> *Leading the spirits and the Elder Ones,*
> *Beauteous and awesome one, aid me I*
> *do ask*
> *In the performance of power, of magic,*
> *of joy, of strength!*

Turn, then, to the oncoming storm, raising both arms out and up, and draw in thirteen breaths deeply, bearing in mind that these breaths draw within power, strength, the lightning, the wind, the storm itself. The magic-worker must project him/herself into the storm, and the storm into oneself . . . becoming truly one with the oncoming tempest.

Think upon that which must be done . . . it may be one thing or it may be many. Call forth into the wind that which is desired, drawing within yourself as one does so, more of the power. Each time the lightning flares especially brightly, send forth in a burst of power, bearing in mind strongly that as the lightning flares and leaps, so also shall the power of magic burst and flare and go forth. That you are pulling forth not only the power which you have drawn into your body, but the power of lightning itself . . . to create, to endure, to radiate everywhere. Bear strongly in mind that the lightning is hereby lending all its vast power.

After each lightning burst, build up again the form of the thought, build up the image of that which is to be accomplished, and at the next large lightning bolt, instantly release that as well. And so on and on, with each bolt and flash of lightning and each peal of thunder, shall magic be sent forth in this manner.

For so long as you desire or are able to, this shall be continued. If you desire to continue performing this magic as the rain falls and the wind gusts, this may be also an especially effective time . . . perhaps the best for such magic.

When you feel that enough has been done, or that your energies are exhausted for the time, call forth in these or similar words:

To the east:
> *I give thee thanks, O winds of storm*
> *O gales of power*
> *That have aided me in this magic!*
> *Go well, and blessings be with you!*
> (Banishing Pentagram)

To the south:
> *I give thee thanks, O lightnings of*
> *storm*
> *Brilliant and searing*
> *That have aided me in this magic!*
> *Go forth, and blessings be with you!*
> (Banishing Pentagram)

To the west:
> *I give thee thanks, O torrents*
> *of rain*
> *Deluging and cleansing*
> *That have aided me in this magic!*
> *Wash free, and wild, and pure,*
> *And blessings be with you!*
> (Banishing Pentagram)

To the north:
> *I give thee thanks, O earth*
> *which moves*
> *And slides with the storm*
> *That has aided me in this magic!*

Rest solid, and blessings be
*   with you!*
(Banishing Pentagram)

Invoke to thank the God, calling into the wind with
arms spread wide:
O great and mighty One,
Thou who hast helped me to use
*   the lightning*
And torrents of the storm
I thank You for aiding me,
For being with me, and one
*   with myself*
In this magic! Blessed Be!

As above, to the Goddess:
O wild and powerful Rider of the
*   storms,*
Thou who dost reveal the deepest
*   of magics.*
I thank you for your presence here
In aiding me, and in being one with
*   myself*
In this magic!
My love and my thanks be with
*   Thee*
O gracious one! Blessed Be!

Then, with arms outspread, call out to the storm itself:
I thank thee, O storm of power
And I salute the life within thee!
In the names of wide-ruling gods
I do give thee thanks, and release!
Evoe he blessed be!
Evoe he blessed be!
Evoe he blessed be!

Depart then as quickly as possible, to rest and to partake of good warm food and drink . . . for this will have
been a strenuous rite!

---

* We strongly suggest that you use adequate precaution when performing this ritual. Pick your ritual spot near a grove of trees or
some object taller than yourself so that the lightning will be
attracted elsewhere. Also, do not use your sword or other metal
objects during heavy lightning activity. It is safest to perform the
entire ritual before the storm reaches your position.

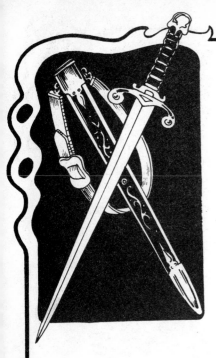

Beacon of Light

Prior to this rite, all shall have been properly prepared through study and meditation, having a concept of the Body of Light. Much background study in mythology is desirable, as well as considerable practice in magic-working of the Bardonian type. Above all, those partaking of this rite shall have a concept and an understanding of the ability to transcend the human state.

The Rite of the Beacon of Light is an experiment in "signalling to the gods" . . . . letting the vast, trans-human and supra-normal matrices of living Power know that you have resolved to advance toward an elevation of soul and spirit which approaches demi-godhood, (based on the mystery tradition that "single is the race of men and gods and from a single source we both draw breath . . . "), and that you desire to receive aid and knowledge from the inner planes.

The creation of a star that is inextricably tied in with the body energies and minds of the group members is based on the magical principle that mental creations in this dimension take on physical reality in other dimensions. The star is both a beacon and a temple, and working spiritually within its core will in time sear away the impurities which cling to the self, leaving only the highest facets of the Soul.

Before beginning, the High Priestess and the High Priest shall review the above with the group and shall discuss it so that these important concepts are fresh in the minds of all. Especially shall it be made clear that in the portion of the rite where the Higher Beings do speak to the minds of all, that as each feels one's own personal voices or visions to be ending, she or he should lower hands downwards so that the High Priest may observe when all have finished, thus to resume the rite.

The altar shall be set to the North or the East with incense, candles and symbols of the female and male aspects of godhood . . . ideally a rose, a lily, and a sword. Thirteen candles shall be set around the periphery of the ritual area.

A period of meditation shall precede the rite. Then for a short while all shall link hands in silence for a preliminary purification of power. In these or similar words shall the purification be guided:

> *Now shall we draw forth from all about us*
> *The Pure White light*
> *Which does pervade the Universe,*
> *Drawing the Power of Light*

Within ourselves,
Through every pore of our
bodies
And building a sunwise circle
of Power.
Growing stronger and ever yet
stronger
As the ever-waxing torrent
Becomes a powerful vortex
Linking earth and sky
With ourselves, guiding, from
the mid-point.

As the flow of pure white
energy grows greater,
It cuts through our bodies,
From foot to head,
From front to back,
Piercing through us,
Carrying away all which is
weak, all which is impure.
Leaving only that which is noble
and godlike.
For this rite of power.

Then there shall follow a period of silence for at least twoscore heartbeats while all silently allow the Power so evoked to perform the purification, to crest, and to fade. When he feels it proper the High Priest shall say:

On this night of Power
Do we commence the building
That shall take us in time
Beyond the stars themselves.
To give us, in time,
The breadth of feeling and of
understanding
Which only gods may know.
And we begin by sending a signal
To the gods themselves.

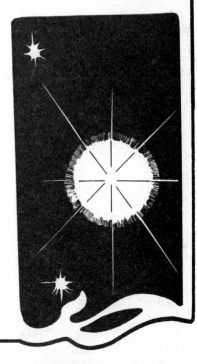

(At this point, an invocation of the elements may be performed, if the group has one it chooses to use, tailored to individual tradition and geographical location. This is optional).
The High Priestess shall then hold out a hand in salute, calling:

All which creates,
Bringing forth and nurturing
  new life,
Infinite and everlasting
Beyond time and beyond space,
Vast matrix of Powers bearing
  true sentience,
Mark well what happens on this
  night!

There shall follow a pause of at least thirteen heartbeats. Then shall the High Priest say to the assembled group:

Let us now commence the chant
To build a vortex of Power and
  of light
More vast than ever before,
For the Gods themselves to recognize.
As we do resound the tones of
  magical evocation,
Let us call forth,
  within and through,
The pure white light which
  does pervade the universe.
Holding within ourselves
  that which is needed
For the duration of the rite
Transmuting us into beings
  of transcendent light.

The High Priestess shall say:
As we do proceed, let us each
Become the magical persona
  of our visions,
Clad in light and radiant
  with Power.
Let us each become, in mind
  and in will,
Demigods who shall ere long
Ascend to the most mighty
  of thrones.

The chant shall be led by the High Priest and the High Priestess until it is felt that Power is being built most strongly, and that all are entering a near-ecstatic state of being. The chant is resounded with strength and with musical tones again and again. A favorite power chant may be selected by the group, or the following simple

chant may be used:
> *Power grow and power come*
> *forth!*

When it is felt that the desired exhalted state of consciousness has been reached, the sudden command shall be given to:
> *Be still!*

There shall be a pause while all do sense the flow of Power which has now been evoked. Then shall the High Priest begin the Narration of the Journey:
> *Feel the pulsing rise of the Power*
> *which we have called forth.*
> *Watch, in your minds' eye*
> *As we ourselves become as if*
> *sculptured in light,*
> *And feel the rising of sheer*
> *strength, beauty, and power*
> *Within every fiber of our being.*
> *See now, in your minds' eye*
> *That the place of our rite is rising,*
> *Turning and turning yet faster*
> *Through the brightening planes of*
> *existence,*
> *Wheeling upwards ever faster*
> *Through all dimensions,*
> *Nearby and far,*
> *Glowing with an intensity*
> *Painful to the mortal eye*
> *But not to ours!*
> *It is as though we have now*
> *Become the very core*
> *Of a new and brilliant star.*
> *Sense and see.*
> *Feel the glow of pulsing Power*
> *As our Star grows ever*
> *stronger.*
> *Repeat now as I call!*

(All repeat after every call):
> WE CALL ON YOU, O GODS!
> SEE US HERE, MARK US WELL,
> BEYOND TIME, BEYOND SPACE,
> FROM THE HEART OF A BRIGHT
> NEW STAR WE CALL THEE!
> KNOW THAT WE ARE HERE,
> FOR WE CALL ON YOU TO AID,

TO HELP US ADVANCE TOWARDS
    AN EXALTED STATE.
KNOW THAT WE ARE HERE,
O MIGHTY ONES,
AND SPEAK TO THE MIND OF
    EACH ONE OF US!

(At this point, there will suddenly be silence for the space of several minutes, as each within the rite listens and hears and sees).

As each feels that his or her vision and words from the Higher Planes has ended, she or he will slowly lower hands to a position of rest. When the High Priest sees that all have finished their contacts, he shall say, in these or similar words:

Now we begin a return from
    whence we came,
Leaving fixed the star which we
    have set in the sky,
Somewhere, somewhen.
This place of ritual will always
    remain here
In the silent, brilliant light
So that each of us can return
At any time to this Temple of
    Stellar Flame.
Each of us shall also draw
    within, and retain,
The Body of Light
Which has here been built,
That it may become stronger
And yet ever stronger
With each and every magical
    operation.
We return to the mundane,
Yet we carry the spark
Of growing Divinity
Within each of our souls.
For each of us should often
    use this great temple
Temple of Power,
And each should use also the
    Body of Light.

All shall be given time to return.

Then shall the High Priestess and the High Priest silently

bless cakes and wine, and silently serve such to all attending. There need be no haste in beginning conversation, but once it is started, all in the rite should tell of what they have seen and heard. Any further talk should be of things divine and transcendent.

When it is felt that the rite should end, the High Priestess shall say:

I say unto you, O friends,
Who are seekers of the highest
Of all paths,
That on this night we have
Begun the greatest of all
    works . . .
The transition to Godhood.
In the far reaches of time and of
    space
We have set forth our new
    star . . .
A beacon to the Gods themselves,
Which shall become ever
    stronger
And more vastly powerful
As time proceeds.
Yet now we must return
To that which is mundane
And end this night of nights.

And as the ritual is closed, shall be said:

This rite is ended. Merry
meet and merry part!

HOW TO MAKE BATH OIL

This recipe is for patchouli bath oil, a fragrance connected with love incense, love sachets and burned for divination. It is a very heady scent and one you will find very appealing.

¼ cup safflower oil   1 dram patchouli oil
1 cup water   2 Tablespoons glycerine
2 teaspoons alkanet dye

Make the alkanet dye by simmering ½ oz. of alkanet root in 1 cup of distilled water for 5 minutes. Mix all of the ingredients together and pour into a special bottle. Use a small amount in your bath. If you need special conditioning for dry skin you can substitute some wheat germ oil for part of the safflower oil. You can also add a small amount of coconut oil directly to the bath water.

HOW TO MAKE DREAM PILLOWS

Dream pillows have been used for centuries to induce certain states of mind or to heal certain ailments. To make the pillow just take a piece of satin (rectangular), fold it in half as shown and sew up two sides. Stuff the pillow with the appropriate herbs and then sew up the final side.

Herbs to induce prophetic dreams: Heliotrope, ash bark, Bay Laurel, Marigold, Rose petals.

To induce sleep: Lemon Balm, Migonette

To banish headaches: Chamomile, Violets, White Lavender, Rosemary, Cowslip.

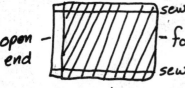

open end — sew — fold — sew
right sides together

turn to right side out and fill with herbs.

open end

sew the final open side.

Magic
Workings

Magical Dance

he Priestess of the Dance should have shielded candles placed at the four quarters and the altar set as usual. After the casting of the circle the alter may be moved to the north edge of the ritual area if she desires. The circle should be as large as needed. Again the size should be determined by the Priestess. Other members of the coven shall sit just inside the edge of the circle.

Music for this rite shall be chosen by the Priestess of the Dance, and shall be appropriate to the aim of the ritual dance. For example, bellydancing music might be used for love or fortune magic, drum solos for protection or for times of psychic attack. Electronic music, flutes, sitar, etc. might be used for deeper magics.

The costume worn for the dance should be chosen for maximum effect on the dancer and on others in the circle. They may be middle-eastern, belly-dancing, ethnic, etc. It should allow completely free movement. It often is useful to have the costume relate in some way to the goal of the dancing rite. Jewelry, particularly if worn over or near the psychic centers, can help in channeling the psychic forces.

The Priestess should perform the style and type of dance which she prefers. Modern dance of various folk forms are useful. Belly-dancing techniques are particularly effective since they stem from an ancient temple style. But if the Dancing Priestess has no formal training, she should improvise as she so desires.

She should make changes and do the dance as she sees fit, since it is the basic pattern only that is of importance.

There must be a balance of women and men present for the rite, and they must be well-trained in magic. All should have at least some familiarity with sex magic, Tantra, or Kundalini. Depending on the work to be accomplished and the feelings of the coven members, sex magic may follow with independent pairs after the rite to increase the effectiveness.

Although the magical dance is intended to be performed with at least one male present, the Priestess may at times wish to perform it alone. In such a case she should have some prominent representation of the male forces in nature. Traditionally a skull-and-crossbones (which need not be human) would be placed on or before the altar, but any masculine image or symbolism which is of particular personal value to the Priestess may be used.

When all is in readiness the Priestess shall proceed

to the center of the circle and stand for a moment, meditating on the goal of the dance magic to be done. Then she shall signal for the music to begin.

The Calling of the Air Elementals

The dance should call and attract with the body of the dancer, and should be done facing to the east most of the time. Summon by swirling the costume or robe, and swaying the body as if in the wind. Attract by smoothing the body, fast and sprightly dance, swirling hair, etc. . . . symbolizing the attributes of air. Use the upper torso of the body.

The Calling of the Fire Elementals

The dance should call and attract with the body of the dancer, and should be done facing towards the south most of the time. Summon by a short fiery dance, then a shimmy in which the body and arms simulate fire. Attract by dancing as if with a body of pure flame. Use head and shoulders.

The Calling of the Water Elementals

The dance should call and attract with the body of the dancer, and should be done facing towards the west most of the time. Summon by a slow sensuous body and passionate dancer symbolizing the attributes of water. Using the abdomen as the bellydancing technique, is appropriate here as the mid section of the body is associated with the water elements.

The Calling of the Earth Elementals

The dance should call and attract with the body of the dancer, and should be done facing towards north most of the time. Summon by a Calypso type dance with short, abrupt movements. Earthy! Use feet and legs, loins, and hips, as these are associated with the earth element.

Then make a brief salute to the east to complete the circle.

Invocation to the Ancient Ones

Take the sword and do a short, swirling dance. Standing before the altar and facing it, do a dancing salute to the God, the Goddess, and the Ancient Ones. The Priestess may do whatever form she considers appropriate here, of which what is given is a sample. Hold the sword upwards over the head in salute and pause for the space of five heartbeats, eyes closed. Then slowly

lower the sword, and body, downwards into a kneeling position, head either down or thrown back.

The first part of the dancing rite has been completed. There may now be a cause for rest.

Magic Workings

Here the dancer can improvise, dancing to symbolize what she particularly desires for herself or for others. The ending of the spell-dance should be fast and dramatic with a definite climax.

Afterwards, she and the others in the circle should relax and partake of refreshments.

The Release of the Air Elementals

This dance should stress breathing and the upper torso, as the air element is related to the lungs and breast. Swirling of the costume, the hair, and generally becoming as the wind is appropriate. Close the dance such that it ends abruptly with the body and arms pointing east, possibly kneeling.

The Release of the Fire Elementals

This should be a short, fiery, dance, perhaps with a shimmy of the body, arms, shoulders, and head to simulate fire. 'Become as fire.' Use head and shoulders, as the fire element is related to this part of the body. Close the dance such that it ends abruptly with the body and arms pointing south, possibly kneeling.

The first part provided a ritual dance to be combined with magical workings. Now we shall discuss some of the theory behind dance magic, and discuss techniques of effectively combining hypnosuggestion and an ecstatic trance state with psychic energy dynamics.

Dancing to Raise Energy—Activating
a Psychic Battery

Any type of physical exercise — and dancing in particular, can engender a tremendous amount of psychic energy. This is attested to by the fact that the human aura can be seen to expand and contract wildly during such activity. The dancer who is aware of the psychic energy flow can use this to advantage.

First of all, it must be understood that the flow of psychic energy operates within a dynamic system. There is, or actually, there should be a harmonious balance between the energy that the dancer sends out and the energy that the dancer draws in. Ideally, such a harmonious relationship should exist between the dancer and her audience — as she dances, the energy she raises with her body is directed at the onlookers, who by their fixed attention and excitement, send back energy to the dancer. She draws the energy back in magnetically as she breathes in, and is thus revitalized. If the dancer is not able to create this energy bond with her audience, she only sends out energy that is lost, and becomes rapidly fatigued by the excessive energy drain on her body. Hence, when a dancer throws off energy, it is imperative that she have a psychic energy source that she can draw from. When a human source is not available, the dancer must be skilled at pulling through energy from the akasthic (cosmic) source. This can be done by the pore-breathing technique, as follows:

Basic Pore-Breathing Technique

As you inhale, breathe in very deeply, visualizing the vital silver-gold-pure white cosmic light being drawn out of the atmosphere — being pulled in with your breath and sucked in through every pore in your body. FEEL the vital energy sweeping through your body. Realize that every cell in the body is thus envigorated. Then, exhale, relaxing as you do so, directing the channelized energy toward whatever goal you have in mind. VISU-ALIZE the energy flowing from your body and being channeled to your desires. Continue to breathe in this energy from the cosmic source, directing it outward as you exhale.

Use of the Elements

Those with an affinity to one of the four elements, (these being fire, earth, air, and water) can call upon these as sources of needed energy. If you are uncertain about elemental affinities, you can check your horoscope to determine whether you have a preponderance of planets in the signs attributed to a particular element. For example, an individual with an abundance of planets in the water signs — Cancer, Scorpio, and Pisces — would probably be successful in tapping magnetic forces (of the water element). Grand trines in any element especially enable the individual to call upon those forces as an energy source.*

When a strong affinity to a particular element is felt, the dance can invoke the Lords of that Quarter; tra-

* See *A to Z Horoscope Maker and Delineator* by Llewellyn George. Llewellyn Publications.

ditionally, fire is in the south, earth is in the northern quarter, air in the east, and water in the west. The dancer proceeds to perform a dance with movements suggestive of that element. See pages 84 and 85.

It is important to remember that a healthy body requires a harmonious balance of the elements, so an imbalance — either an over-or-under abundance of any one of the elements — can be harmful. If the dancer calls upon a particular element excessively, she should compensate for the other elements later on. Frequently, however, conscious action is not necessary as one's own unique metabolism often makes the adjustments automatically.

However, some individuals suffer chronically from metabolic imbalances of the elements, and when this is the case, the magical dance can be applied to correct these problems. For example, an individual suffering from nervous disorders due to an excess of affinity to the air element could call upon the earth element for strength and calm. An individual suffering from negative effects of the water element, such as congestion, edema, etc. could use the magical dance to charge the body with the fire element, to help balance the conditions. The basic idea behind this is to realize what the nature of the imbalances are, and then to correct them by applying a larger dose of the element lacking.

Other Applications of the Magical Dance

The Magical Dance has many applications once the dancer understands the basic theory behind it.

A very excellent idea is to perform a general dance upon rising each morning. Such a dance would be specifically designed to generate good health and build up of energy, strength, and positive attitudes by consciously pulling in and sending out "good vibes" — causing a state of "serendipity."

An energy raising dance is particularly desirable if performed immediately prior to a ritual. In such an instance, the dancer stores the built up energy in her body — in some ways similar to the way in which a group raises a cone of power — and retains it until a latter part of the ritual where the energy is released and directed toward the specific goal of the rite.

Certain elements of general rituals, such as the calling of the quarters could be altered into semi-dance steps suggestive of the intention! In other words, a ritual which employs some dance movements, but which is not actually a magical dance in itself.

It is possible to imbue specific amulets with power via the dance ritual. This could be applied towards charging magical tools and amulets. It could also be applied towards charging such diverse items as love letters and job application forms. It just takes imagination to list what kind of objects could be so used!

Basically, what this all amounts to is that any kind of magical spell can be used in combination with a dance suggestive of what is desired. It all depends upon your imagination!

Dance and Trance

The other major aspect of the dance ritual is that the dance is an effective means of attaining altered states of consciousness and an ecstatic trance-like state.

Ecstatic dance has long been important to many religions in other societies of the world — especially shamanistic type religions — among them the voudon religion and many of the Amerindian cults.* This principle is also to be found traditionally in many Wiccan rituals where circumambulations are combined with dance steps to bring the entire coven into an hypnotic state. Gerald Gardner was particularly interested in these methods.

It is possible to use the ecstatic dance-trance to heighten the individual's psychic awareness and receptivity by bringing her into a closer contact with the subconscious mind; and also by being so receptive, to be able to raise power by channeling the primitive emotions and forces drawn out of the depths of the unconscious mind. Among the many psychic abilities that would be enhanced would be clairvoyance and the ability to perceive the aura, clairaudience, telepathy, precognition, psychomancy, etc. etc. Indeed, frequent practice of the magical dance could help to loosen physical bonds and facilitate astral projection. On a much higher level, the ecstatic trance can be used to bring forth the archetypical personalities to speak through the individual, and even carry the ecstatic individual through the astral realms and bring her into personal contact and realization of Goddesshood.

For these reasons, the magical dance could be performed by individuals to great effect immediately prior to certain rituals, most notably the Calling Down the Moon, where the Priestess or other participants are

* See *Voudoun Fire* by Denning & Phillips, Llewellyn Publications.

especially required to work in a trance-like state.

As a final note on this subject, caution is urged—the individual should be aware of her capabilities and of the amount of power that is in her capacity to handle, taking care not to over-extend herself until a proper degree of adeptness is attained.

And, one additional word on the magical dance... Performing the Dance of Power has a fortuitous side effect in that it builds up sexual magnetism. With the power thus released, the individual develops greater confidence in all of her abilities. A more positive frame of mind is thus engendered with accompanying good feelings which help to perpetuate such a positive mind and a state of continuing good fortune. So remember—

THINK SENSUAL!

THINK SEXY!

THINK MAGICAL!

Here is an outlined list of suggestions of some basic movements which can be symbolically applied to a magical dance working. This list is provided merely to stimulate the imagination, for the actual possibilities are, of course, unlimited. Most of these movements are belly dance movements, however, readers who are knowledgable of the dance will certainly come up with many interesting alternates, variations, or elaborations to be used in personal magical renditions.

For additional information, the reader may wish to refer to *The Complete Belly Dancer,* by Julie Russo Mishkin and Marta Schili (New York: Doubleday, 1973), and the *Serena Technique of Belly Dancing,* by Serena and Alan Wilson (New York: Drake, 1972). Much of our material and terminology has been drawn out of these books, which are very popular source material on this subject.

GENERAL ENERGY DYNAMICS

Try hand movement combinations with emphasis on drawing energy in through your left hand and sending it fourth through your right. Always use this in combination with psychic energy "pore-breathing" techniques. Visualizations of red-gold-silver energy flowing through the body with movements which focus energy on specific chakras is good. Consciously expand your aura and extend it to the audience. Draw energy off attentive people of the audience and pull it through your pores.

TO INDUCE TRANCE

Begin with slow repetitious or fast movements

(which may bring about hyperventilation). Sway, swirl, or spin, remembering to keep your attitude psyched up! With total mental and emotional involvement, you concentrate on the fixed desire.

SUMMONING THE FIRE ELEMENT
Have very fast movements in your dance, using such techniques as leaping with arms above your head, vigorous spins, kicks, spinning kicks, fast hip shimmies, fast shoulder shimmies, running step shimmy (Tahitian shimmy), Turkish arm pose.

SUMMONING THE EARTH ELEMENT
Basic ground work is required in this dance. Doing such things as zill work along the ground. Or perhaps back-bends and back bends going to the floor. You can use movements which accentuate hips, perhaps pushing your hips forward as in Egyptian basic. The hip may be thrust, slide and hands may also be used to draw attention to the hips. Figure-eight sways and half-moon movements can be done. These same movements can be done with a dip and are especially good for 'grounding' power, possibly using a pivot bounce or basic walk.

SUMMONING THE AIR ELEMENT
The movements here emphasize veil work. Doing such things as veil turning or suggestive veil twirling. Accentuate upper extremities, using such arm positions as: willowy arm movements, arms above head, basic (classic) arms, Cleopatra (snake) arms. Use large or small shoulder circles. Also fast shoulder thrusts, stomach flutters, and rib cage circles can be done.

SUMMONING THE WATER ELEMENT
Turn slowly with the veil in these movements. Use suggestive twirling of the veil. Work can be done behind the veil, with basic arm movements, Cleopatra (snake) arms, finger movements, even finger ripples. Use undulations, drawing attention to rolling belly movements. Slow rib cage slides, slow shoulder thrust, arms far out at the sides with slowed movements can be done with snakey movements. Floor work is also suggested.

PROPS
Props are very important to the performance. These may include appropriately colored veils, knives and swords used in air element dance, candles used in fire dances, interesting arrangements of battery-powered

lights are possible and especially effective when used in a headdress. Use of canes or quarter staffs is very suggestive of air or earth elements. Foot jewelry can especially accentuate earthy movements, and coins are also symbolic of the earth element.

eek a place of peace and tranquility, and spend a while relaxing both mind and body.

Then a pause of no less than five breaths shall be taken while the body and mind are relaxed and made receptive. Then reach downwards towards the feet with hands open and fingers spread, exhaling. Slowly rise straight, drawing in a deep breath, and slowly bringing the open hands up from the direction of the feet to the personal center (womb or solar plexus region), as if drawing forth some insubstantial nimbus of Power from the ground, up through the feet and legs, and up into the body's center.

You must strongly feel, or attempt to feel, the almost ecstatic sensation of the growing energy as it rises and is held within the center of the body.

Hold the Power for a long moment, then release your breath slowly and completely as your hands and arms are smoothly and slowly brought out from the center until they extend directly out from the body in either direction.

You should strongly feel, ar attempt to feel, the very pleasing sensation of the Power flowing out from the body through your arms and spreading out to infinity from the outstretched fingertips.

This exercise should be performed at first with no particular thought in mind . . . merely keeping a tranquil openness with all things as your ideal.

Then, after perhaps five to nine sessions, you should begin to visualize—and visualize strongly and completely—that which you deeply desire. Yet remember: keep it within the realm of possibility!

Magic is accomplished with the Power thus sent forth . . . with a strongly visualized goal and a driving feeling of ecstasy to shape and bend the patterns of existence.

Building the Flow of the Force

Spell of the Comb and Mirror

agic comes forth from the hair. Ancient legend tells again and again of the enchant- ress who sings as she brushes her hair by moonlight, weaving a powerful spell as she does so. In Central Europe and in the Germanic lands, this theme recurs often. One small but exquisite example which I cannot resist quoting, is a passage from Heinrich Heine's rendering of archaic legend in 'The Lorelei':

> . . . . . The air is cool and twilight
> Flows down the quiet Rhine;
> A mountain alone in the high light
> Catches the faltering shine.
>
> One rosy peak half gleaming
> Reveals, enthroned in air,
> A goddess, lost in dreaming,
> Who combs her golden hair.
>
> With a golden comb she is combing
> Her hair, as she sings a song;
> Heard and reheard through the gloaming,
> It hurries the night along.
>
> The boatman has heard what has bound him
> In throes of a strange, wild love,
> He is blind to the reefs that surround him,
> Who sees but the vision above . . . . . .

For power can be drawn in, and set forth again, through the hair, after being shaped by deep concentration and the steady rhythm of comb or brush. On the Continent, Witches in working their magic, or ordinary women doing simple folk spells for security of home, freedom from illness, or fertility of the crops, would have their long hair loose and unbound. It helped greatly. Jakob Grimm's massive sourcebook, 'Teutonic Mythology,' is replete with literally hundreds of examples from Continental myth, custom, and folklore.

Combing was not the only way to render magic. All across Europe, at one time or another, the custom of fertility rites existed in which women would dance nude in the fields, shaking their long hair and swirling it about. Such methods were used in association with wind magic, of which a charming example is given in Grimm's fairy tale, 'The Goose Girl'. When the heroine wants to be alone, she calls, 'Blow, blow, thou gentle wind, I say, blow Conrad's little hat away, and make him chase it

here and there, until I have braided all my hair, and bound it up again.'

The Spell of the Comb and Mirror

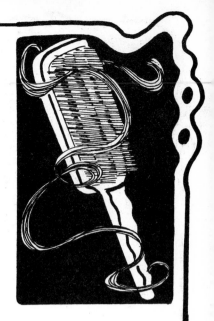

At such time as a woman feels that for pleasure, rest, or for magical need she wishes to draw power and strength to herself, she shall draw it to her by the brushing or combing of her hair. If brush, comb, and mirror of silver be available, she should use them, though it is of importance primarily that her implements be closely linked with her.

She shall dress in a manner which is auspicious to this spell, and sit comfortably alone, dimming the lights of her chamber. A single candle should be lit, of a color fitted to her goal, along with a sweet incense. For the space of thirteen heartbeats or for several minutes or more as she feels proper, she should meditate and become quiet within herself. Then take up a comb, or brush, saying aloud or within herself with each stroke:

O Lady of shimmering beauty,
For whom the stars are shinning jewels,
And the universe Her creation and plaything,
Weaver of destinies
And protectress of things wild and free.
Make me now, I do ask
To be thy sister.
Make me one with thee
And grant me thy far-flung power.
Grant to this, thy Witch and Sorceress
Strength within and without
As eternal as the boundless sea;
The calm assurance of my powers
To make any do my bidding
And the winds, waters, and fires,
The hills themselves
Lend willingly themselves to me,
Give to me, who am of thy ancient Craft
The wisdom of ages, the lore of eons
Knowledge of light, knowledge of dark.
Grant me beauty ever more perfect
That I may reflect thee better.
Build magic within me,
Build power within me.

And the last portion to be repeated for as long as seems proper:

Power be drawn, and power come,
And make me one with thee
Make me greater, make me better.
Grant me strength and grant me power.

O Goddess who is my friend and sister,
I give you love and thanks
O Beautiful One.
May the magic I have summoned
Return the stronger when I have need of it.
May wisdom, strength, and comeliness
Remain with me, growing ever finer.
So mote it be!

She shall continue brushing her hair in silence, meditating on what she has spoken or thought, feeling power flow into her with every stroke while every fiber of her body is made vital and strong. She may wish to hum some song of beauty and strength which means much to her.

If she has magic to work she shall think on it at this time, and state it in her own words as she continues to use comb and mirror. She may prefer simply to strengthen and develop her own capabilities. The singing or humming should be continued. Finally she should say:

The spell is ended.

She should kiss her hand towards some nearby image of the Goddess or towards the moon, and should continue brushing or combing until she feels that any excess energy has been sent forth. Then the candle is put out and she says:

The Rite is closed.

Magical Omens

Many omens were formerly derived from the burning of a candle. In the northern counties, a bright spark in the candle-flame was said to predict the arrival of a letter, and if it dropped on the first shake, it was taken as an indication that the missive had already been posted.

The itching of the palm of the right hand is supposed to signify that it will shortly receive money, whereas if the left hand be irritable, it is an indication that before many days money will have to be paid away.

St. Austin says that the custom of blessing persons when they sneeze goes back to the pre-Christian era, and that the ancients were wont to go back to bed again if they sneezed while putting on their shoes.

(from The Hand of Destiny—The Folklore
and Superstitions of Everyday Life
C.J.S.Thompson, Singing Tree Press, 1970)

Building an Astral Temple

 his operation requires perhaps thirty minutes initially, while resting undisturbed in some quiet place . . . preferably your own bedroom. Before starting, use an athame or wand to draw a triple circle about the place where you will be lying (moving clockwise within the circle), and place a candle at each of the four cardinal points. . . . Place a small image of the Goddess above your head or somewhere nearby. Raise the athame or wand in salute towards the image and say:

> *In the name of the Gracious Goddess*
> *And the God who is her consort.*
> *May that which is left within this circle*
> *Remain safe and secure*
> *Within the protection of the Lady*
> *And of the God*
> *While I am away.*

Touch your wand or athame to your lips and hold it out in salute to the Goddess and the God.

Lie down, close your eyes, and relax for a few moments, allowing your mind to become calm and serene. Imagine then that you are exuding your astral body out through the top of your head and leaving your body relaxed and remaining behind. Picture yourself standing next to your body, and at all times strive to transfer as much of your consciousness as possible into your astral self. Feel the floor beneath your feet; when you reach out for something, make the feel of it as vivid as possible.

Look towards the eastern wall of the room, picturing there a door of archaic design. With your imagination, walk to the door, swing it open, and pass through. The land you picture on the other side should be some remote place where you will be alone, yet a place where you can feel completely at home, in contact with nature, and close to the Gods. It may be a seashore, mountain crag, or whatever. Look back at the *other* side of the entry door, noting its location . . . in a rock outcropping, a hillock, or a fragment of an ancient wall. Note also that you can, through imagination, array yourself in the most ornate clothes, the most magical costume, or nothing at all. Yet remember to hold yourself in normal human shape and walk one step at a time. This clear and consistent visualization is important.

You may prefer to imagine that an ancient temple is already near your entry portal, awaiting your use. If so, you should add a few touches with your own hands to truly make it your own. On the other hand, you may prefer to grant yourself the strength of a demigod to cut and carry and fit the stones with your own hands, building a massive stone henge or a great, classically simple hall. Whatever the case, the temple should face east and sunlight or moonlight should fall upon the altar.

When you are finished, imagine yourself standing before the altar and consecrating the temple to the Goddess and to the God with a heartfelt rite of your own composing. If such is your desire, grant yourself the power to bring down magical fire for an eternal altar flame, or to place a glowing nimbus of light about shrine and altar.

Then imagine clearly your walking from the temple to the entry door, returning through it to your room, and back into your body through the top of your head. Arise and with wand or athame break the circle and thank the Lady and the God for their protection.

Once an astral temple has been built, you should use it frequently for devotional purposes and for performing such rites as you desire . . . every evening at first and at least at New and Full Moon thereafter. (You should keep the phase of the Moon over your astral temple to be about the same as in the everyday world.)

At first you should physically draw the protective circle in your room, light the candles, and evoke the Lady's protection before each journey . . . though increasingly the journey will be more of a genuine astral experience. After a time you may forego the material ceremony and instead perform it in your imagination (or astral) before going out through the door and again upon your return.

After some practice you should ideally spend a few minutes just after going to bed and just before falling asleep, visiting your temple. Try to return before falling asleep, otherwise you will probably do a considerable amount of "astral wandering" before awakening. Although this wandering is pleasant and interesting, it is wise to develop and keep a strong self-discipline in your magical operations.

In visiting your astral temple, it is well to always picture yourself alone. Ultimately others will begin to appear, and such visitors must be allowed to come, and later to speak, without any "pushing" from yourself. After a time, however, they will choose to speak and give you certain information. This will lead to some very rewarding and enlightening experiences. This will be something unique to you alone.

Spell of the Five Candles

 or this magical operation it is useful to have a five-stick candelabrum, made with one candle at the center and four others placed equally about it. Lacking this implement, it is acceptable to improvise by placing one candle at the center and the other four in the quarters about it, placed relatively closely on the floor or tabletop.

The candelabrum should be placed at the center of the coven, with its arms oriented to the quarters. At the east should be a yellow candle to symbolize the element of Air, at the south a red candle to symbolize Fire, at the west a blue candle for Water, and at the north a green candle for Earth. In the center should be a pure white candle to symbolize the Divine Force of the Goddess and the God. A taper should be provided for igniting the candles and a snuffer for extinguishing them. A censer with incense, a clean, white, unused piece of paper and a collection of various color fiber-point pens should be nearby.

For dramatic effect it may be desired to use a small portion of flash powder comprised of equal portions sugar and saltpeter well mixed, and a pinch of calendala or other herbal condenser added.

When all are prepared to begin the spell of healing all other lights shall be put out and the coven all link hands to put their minds into an even and serene, meditative manner, clearing away all thoughts of the mundane world. Incense should be lit. Then shall the Priestess light the taper, saying in these or similar words:

This rite of healing has begun.
Let us now call the elements
And welcome the Great Ones.

She hands the taper to the one chosen for air, who lights the yellow candle, saying:

We call upon you,
O creatures of air,
And bid you welcome
Among us here
In this spell of healing.
Blessed Be!
All: BLESSED BE!

The taper is passed to the one chosen for fire, who lights the red candle, saying:

We call upon you,
O creatures of fire,
And bid you welcome
Among us here
In this spell of healing.
Blessed Be!
All: BLESSED BE!

The taper is passed to the one chosen for water, who
lights the blue candle, saying:

We call upon you,
O creatures of water,
And bid you welcome
Among us here
In this spell of healing.
Blessed Be!
All: BLESSED BE!

The taper is passed to the one chosen for earth, who
lights the green candle, saying:

We call upon you,
O creatures of earth,
And bid you welcome
Among us here
In this spell of healing.
Blessed Be!
All: BLESSED BE!

The taper is passed to the man chosen to welcome the
God. He touches the taper to the central white candle
but does not light it as he says:

We welcome you, good friend,
God of forest and of stream,
Guardian of joy and of strength,
We ask your presence now
In this spell of healing.
Blessed Be!
All: BLESSED BE!

The taper is passed to the woman chosen to welcome
the Goddess. She touches the central, white candle to
flame as she says:

We welcome you, O beautiful one,
Goddess of the vast starry sky,

Giver of wisdom and of magic.
We ask your presence now
In this spell of healing.
Blessed Be!
All: BLESSED BE!

At this time the member of the coven who is closest to the person being healed should explain in detail the nature of the malady and the type of healing which is required. Also, the one to be healed should be described at length such that all in the circle may form a vivid and accurate picture of the subject in their minds and even feel that they have formed a rapport with him or her. If a photograph is available it should be passed around for all to see, then carefully placed at the base of the candelabrum.

Then shall the Priestess or Priest bid the coven to be silent, and take out the paper and colored pens. Some representation of the person to be healed shall be sketched and symbols of healing marked in. Then the paper and pens should be passed deosil to the next person who shall then add her or his own depiction of healing, then pass it on to the next and so on.

Each Witch's additions to the healing symbolism should be that which is felt to be strong and efficacious: one might sketch in the traditional triple circle of protection about the figure of the one to be healed, another might add the proper colors being directed in to heal the aura (and the body within), someone might sketch the traditional Egyptian figure of Lady Isis with her wings of protection spread, and so on.

The paper should go twice about the circle for additions to be made (and silence shall be maintained all this time), then passed yet a third time so that all might see the final work. Then shall the Priest or Priestess fold the paper several times; if flash powder is used, perhaps a teaspoon of it should be placed within the folded sheet. Then shall the corner of the folded sheet be lit at the white candle and stuffed into the incense brazier as the Priest or Priestess says:

The power and the strength
Which we have placed in this drawing
Shall now go forth
As does this smoke and flame.
Healing shall be effected,
Complete and total,
By the power of the Elements
And by the will of the Gods.

If flash powder is used, there shall be a pause until the bright flare and the smoke subside; if not, until the paper is consumed. Then shall be said:

So mote it be!
All: SO MOTE IT BE!

The one who at the beginning of the spell had lit the candle of Air shall now take the candle snuffer and put out that same candle saying:

We do thank you,
O creatures of Air,
For granting your healing powers.
Go now in peace,
And with our blessings.
Blessed Be!
All: BLESSED BE!

The candle snuffer shall then be passed to the one who had summoned Fire, and the above shall be repeated for Fire. Likewise also shall the elements of Water and Earth be released as their candles are put out. The Priest shall then touch the snuffer to the central candle without putting it out, saying:

O hearty and Powerful One,
Patron of healing
And friend of all which lives,
We thank you for your presence here.
Blessed Be!
All: BLESSED BE!

Then shall the Priestess take the snuffer and put out the central candle, saying:

O gracious Lady,
Giver of peace and serenity
And of renewal,
We thank you for your presence here.
Blessed Be!
All: BLESSED BE!

There shall be a pause of five heartbeats, and the Priestess shall say:

This spell is ended.
Merry meet and Merry part.
All: MERRY MEET AND MERRY PART.

Pathworking

Inner-plane journeys or "pathworkings" are both a technique for training the mind for actual astral travel. Indeed, when used by those who are well experienced in magic and meditation, an inner-plane journey can readily become an astral journey.

Numerous pathworkings are to be found in the Book of Shadows and other sources. Coven members may, however, create their own journeys; in such cases it is best to use mythological or archetypal material, being certain that the resulting journey is entirely consistent with its sources. Inner-plane workings which clash with basic human archetypes will cause profound psychological and magical troubles.

The one conducting the exercise, be it Priestess, Priest, or simply the group member most talented at narration, should be totally familiar with any inner-plane journey undertaken. Attention must be given, and mention made, concerning major events and appearances at the times and places where they would logically first be perceived. Do not, for example, describe a tower or archway in detail . . . then last of all tell the color, which should have been perceived at a far distance or from the first glance. In short, the narrator should not cause his or her listeners to mentally erase and backtrack, as this would lessen their concentration and damage the effect of the inner-plane working.

Except with very advanced covens it is wise to avoid the Crone Aspect, that is, dark, dangerous, and threatening areas . . . such as journeys into the underworld or dealing with the left-hand path in any form. The mental stability and psychic defenses of all group members must be equal to or better than the challenge offered by any inner-plane working which they undertake. Risks should be taken only in matters of grave importance.

It is well to be remembered also that each member of the group will, during any journey, probably view the surroundings somewhat differently. A good indication of psychism at work during an exercise will be when several persons perceive exactly the same images or sensations. This type of synchronicity should be strived for because it develops closer mental links between the group members, as well as heightening sensitivity. It is also common for various individuals to "wander off" during the course of a pathworking and depart considerably from the route of travel, returning to the rest of the group from time to time. These persons may indeed see other places and other events of importance which will be interesting and enlightening to the rest of the group, even to the narrator. Such ramblings should be described for all once the pathworking is completed. However, the narrator himself should never wander, but remain in full command of the situation.

A major value of such journeys is to visit the Great Archetypes "in person" to seek greater understanding of very basic and fundamental truths. Advanced magical techniques of considerable strength and effectiveness may be learned and utilized on the inner planes. Advanced students and initiates with much experience can gain much from such workings. Particularly powerful inner-plane workings for magical purposes are, of course, best done by volunteer groups of highly-trained members.

It is desirable that the narrator have some familiarity or some background in hypnotism, as this aids greatly in the effectiveness of inner-plane journeying. Smoothness and expressiveness of voice, the ability to weave an atmosphere and maintain it, vividness of description to evoke clear and dramatic visual imagery . . . these are important characteristics.

In preparation for an inner-plane working a proper environment must be created. Candlelight and incense, perhaps light from a fireplace, telephones off the hook, cuckoo clocks silenced, pets out of the house or at least away from the group. Infants and children too small to maintain the tight discipline of silence and stillness should be totally out of earshot. Even soft music might be distracting. No one even the least influenced by alcohol (lightheaded or tipsy) should be allowed to take the journey. And particularly, drugs have no place whatsoever in such workings. Nothing should interfere with the purity of the inner experience sought after.

When all is in readiness the members of the group should relax in the area as the matter of the pathworking is discussed. The narrator should describe the background and aspects important to the working, though it is not necessary to tell the members in advance of the itinerary and imagery. Questions and discussion should be encouraged. Individuals should be advised not to get up quickly after (or during) the working, as dizziness and headache and other problems can result from the shock of breaking out of the super-relaxed semi-hypnotic state too quickly. Also, they should be advised to stay awake and alert in spite of the very relaxed environment, since it is very easy to fall asleep during such operations.

Nothing bad can result from this, however, and indeed one who falls asleep often still completes the entire journey, though with the unconscious part of her or his mind, and of course with no conscious remembrance.

When there are no further questions or comments, the narrator instructs all to relax totally (most prefer to stretch out on couches or on carpeted floors, often under light blankets or in warm robes), to close their eyes, and to let their minds drift and wander. This suggestion is repeated several times, and all are told to take several deep breaths and to relax totally and completely. In an even, steady and soft voice the narrator then gives the sort of relaxation suggestions which he or she personally knows best. Suggestions are given that various sections of the body be relaxed, feel heavy, and totally at ease. Starting with the feet, and spending perhaps a minute or so thus suggesting total relaxation, then repeating the process on up through knees, thighs, hips, torso, shoulders and neck (particularly important!), arms, and hands. Alternately, or additionally, all in the coven should be given porebreathing exercises — first of Earth, to gradually concentrate the earth element in their bodies and become very, very heavy and massive, then dissipate the earth element and similarly breathe the air-element, becoming lighter and lighter yet, then dissipating the air element back and becoming normal. The narrator then should pause and allow as much as half a minute of total silence, then begin narrating the journey. He or she should not wander. Most such inner-plane workings normally take between 20 and 40 minutes.

After completion of the journey or path-working the narrator should allow some time for group members to rouse themselves, then to describe each one's feelings and elicit the experiences of all others in the group. After all have had a chance to tell their particular visions and experiences, coffee or some other mild stimulant should be served to "shut down" the psychic sensitivities and keep individuals awake to make the journey home.

Audience with the Sea Queen

close their eyes
g, slow breaths
She or he will
After thirteen
or more breaths begun, much like the
following:

It is night. We open the door of our cabin and see that the moon is full, though there are some clouds in the sky. We step outside and close the wooden door; the night is cool and the air is slightly damp, with the scent of the sea on it.

On either side in the distance rise forest-covered mountains, and before us a rising, grassy meadow that on the other side slopes down to the sea-cliffs.

Far off over the meadow we can hear the faint sound of the distant surf. All is quiet and serene. We walk away from the cabin on the path that goes on up the hillside, hearing the soft sound of the wind in the tall grass . . . "

(The following outlines the rest of the rite and should be described as the speaker sees it and leads the others.)

Follow the path as it goes up over the hilltop; from there down toward the cliffs.

As we approach the seacliffs, we see that we are perhaps two or three hundred feet above the ocean. We come to the edge and pause, looking down at the waves breaking on the smooth, wide, empty beach below us.

Off to the left, not too far off, we see a dirt road which angles down from the clifftop along the face of the sea cliff. We take this, feeling the sand and rocks beneath our feet, and hearing the ever-louder sound of the waves as we descend along the steep cliff.

We reach the bottom of the dirt path and walk out onto the sandy beach. The sand is dry at first, but damp as we walk further on towards the surf. The moonlight glistens on the sea, and the crests of the waves are white in the full moon.

The shadows of the clouds are noticeable out on the water, and it looks as though some mist or fog is forming not too far out. We turn and pick our way back along the rocks to the beach.

We walk on up the beach, just at the point where the waves wash the furthest up on the sand. The breeze is soft and cool, and the waves are lesser now. The mist

flows its first tendrils about us as we walk, and begins to
thicken as we realize a fog bank has reached us and is
getting ever more dense. The fog is wet, moving only
little; we can no longer see the cliffs or the sea, but only
our own feet and the sand right around us.

We have a strong desire to turn towards the sea . . .
it is as though we hear a soft voice, barely audible,
calling to us over the waters, we turn toward the sea
and continue walking.

The fog is thicker now, though brightly lit by the
full moonlight. The fog swirls about us and over us. We
continue on, and the fog swirls and washes about us,
moving our bodies a little, as though it were dense.

We realize now we are beneath the sea, walking on
out along a bright path of sand, with seaweed, and sea-
grasses on either side. The water does not hinder us, and
we breathe easily, though in a manner somehow different
than before.

Drifting jellyfish with beautiful colored tendrils; it
will not hurt us. We continue.

We notice movement near us, and see that a school
of small, many-colored fish are following behind and beside us. They are curious and friendly.

Oysters in beds next to the path. The light from
overhead is dimmer, but the path is brighter, and there
is a pale luminescence to the path and in the seaweed
about us. Large, white-looking rocks off to either side.

A smooth, large, silver shape moves on overhead to
look at us, then turns and heads away; it is a large shark,
but it is a friend.

As we continue, the light from overhead grows yet
dimmer, but the luminescent flow about us remains and
grows brighter. We can see what look like occasional
ruined stone buildings off to either side as we continue.

The shark swims easily overhead once more, and
vanishes. Off to the side we see a small octopus, its body
luminescing like a rainbow.

The path goes quite close to the wreck of an old
sailing ship. It is empty and quite serene. Were we to
look through an empty porthole we might see things of
value within, but we do not pause. Fish of all sizes are
about us as we continue.

The ruins are all about us now, and the path glows
brightly. Oysters nearby have some shells open, and we
can see the rainbow luminescence within them, and perhaps an occasional pearl. Many fish.

The path goes into the ruin of a great building.
There seems to be no roof on it, and it is draped with

seaweed. *We go in through a large door and find ourselves in a hall strewn with the gold and jewels and treasures of the ages. A scene of incredible richness and splendor. In the midst of it is a throne. We see someone thereon, and approach it.*

The Sea-Queen sits on her throne, dressed in long, flowing white robes that drift about her. Her hair is long and golden, drifting freely about her head, and she wears rich golden jewelry and pearls. She watches us as we approach. She is unhumanly beautiful, with very pale skin. One has the feeling that her emotions and thoughts are not entirely those of a human being.

Before the throne is an altar. This we approach, and pause before it, and bow deeply.

At this point, she will smile and speak . . . but each will hear differently.

When the Queen is done speaking, we bow low once again, and when we rise, the throne is empty. We look about once more at her rich palace.

Out of the great ruined palace. Past the oyster beds.

The fish are dropping away from us. The jellyfish off to the side. Brighter overhead.

Past the ruin of the old wooden ship. More glow from above.

Whiteness swirls about us. We feel it much at first, then less.

Sounds are lesser, water has become fog. We turn back along the shore, fog thins. Fog fades and blows away. We see moonlight and ocean.

Up the path that leads up the cliff-face; we do not tire.

Full moon, the ocean, soft breeze with a touch of salt spray.

We continue up along the path through the meadow. Tall grass.

Over the crest of the hill. Forested mountains to either side.

Our cabin. Bright. Warm. Enter. We are home.

All shall remain silent for a few moments, then awaken fully and compare experiences and impressions. Then all shall relax, have refreshments, and talk as they please.

Earth
Magic

American Indian Ceremonial Prelude

hen all are prepared for ritual, the High Priest and High Priestess shall draw out a sand-altar for the celebrants, explaining the symbolism as they do so.

The High Priest shall have a horn sounded. Then, holding his staff aloft, shall call:

> *At this time and in this place*
> *Do we call upon the Spirits of the*
> *Land*
> *As well as the Mighty Ones of the*
> *Skies.*
> *We call upon the Gods of our own*
> *distant past*
> *From lands far away.*
> *We call upon the Gods of our spiritual*
> *brethren*
> *Who once called these mountains and*
> *this desert*
> *Their own.*

Then shall the High Priestess call:

> *As on high holidays did they*
> *Call to the Gods for that which*
> *was needed,*
> *So also do we.*
> *In this, the harsh season*
> *Of these vast lands*
> *Do we send out our calls*
> *As did they,*
> *In chants of three!*

In what follows, the Priest shall call first, then the Priestess, and finally the celebrants.

> *O great Hunter of the summer sky*
> *Patron and friend, hero and*
> *inspiration,*
> *O Star-Maidens who dance*
> *Through the eternal skies,*
> *Bringers of fruitfulness*
> *And takers of that which has passed*
> *living.*
> *Laughing Coyote.*
> *You who treasure joking*
> *And magic, and adventure.*
> *Friend of humankind.*

Wise Eagle, symbol
And inspiration
Of our highest nature.

O Puma and Yunakat, and
* Rattlesnake,*
Ancient spirits of this land,
Come again as of old
Into this, thy own land,
And walk again upon thy
* high places.*

Look favorably upon our
* dance*
And upon our song
As you did in ages past . . .
For our red friends,
Sisters and brothers to us
* spiritually,*
Who once held this land,
And who, in the dreaming-
* time,*
We may still know.

At this point shall commence the Rite for Earth Cleansing.
(Or other rite, as desired)

Earth-Cleansing

his rite is best accomplished out-of-doors and in a place away from dense human habitation, though of course need and intent of the coven will ultimately be the deciding factor.

The place of the rite shall be large enough to comfortably accomodate all who will be participating. Candles shall be placed at all quarters, in glass jars to shield them from the wind if the ritual is outdoors. Thirteen stone blocks shall be set around the outside edge of the circle. At the center shall be a natural symbol of the Goddess and a representation of the God . . . a large shell or flowers for the Lady and antlers or other animal horns for the God would be appropriate. Two candles or torches shall be set by the representations of the Deities. Pine or similar incense and a censer shall be within the ritual area, and some organic oil for anointing.

Prior to the rite all shall partake of lustral baths, bearing in mind that the bathing is not only cleansing the body, but purifying the soul as well. If robes are worn they should be freshly cleaned.

(Although the salutations to the various aspects of the Goddess and God are here written to be done by the Priestess and the Priest, this may be done by five separate members of the coven if such is desired.)

When all is in readiness the Witches shall gather in the ritual area, and the Priestess shall light the candles or torches by the altar. All shall sit in silence, meditating on the harm done to Nature by centuries of misuse of Nature's resources. During the meditation all people are to sit next to the Earth, endeavouring to feel the chthonic powers moving up within them, and growing in strength. Appropriate readings may be done by various members, allowing a minute or two of silence between readings for all to consider what has been said. All should also think upon the world made new, cleansed of the excesses of present and past generations.

The Priestess shall then take the oil and silently anoint the Goddess and God symbols, and the stones which encompass the ceremonial area. Then she shall silently anoint the men in the rite, and the Priest anoint the women. Then shall the Priestess stand and, facing to the West, raise her arms and say:

At this time and at this place:
Do we meet before the Old Gods
To call for the cleansing of the
Earth,

The purification of land,
    sea, and sky,
And for a return to Nature!
O Sentinels of the Quarters,
Take now your places!

Those who are chosen to be Sentinels of the Quarters shall go to their respective positions. The Sentinel of the East shall place light at that quarter and hold arms out and crossed while facing east. The Sentinel shall call:

Be ye banished, foul vapors
And noxious fumes
Of men's careless works.
For the Earth must be
    made new!

The Sentinel of the South shall place light at that quarter and hold arms out and crossed while facing south. The Sentinel shall call:

Be ye banished, smoky fires of soot
And feverish heats
Of men's careless works.
For the Earth must be
    made new!

The Sentinel of the West shall place light at that quarter and hold arms out and crossed while facing west. The Sentinel shall call:

Be ye banished, seeping vitriol
And foul fluids
Of men's careless works.
For the Earth must be made new!

The Sentinel of the North shall place light at that quarter and hold arms out and crossed while facing north. The Sentinel shall call:

Be ye banished, poisons of soil
And ever-spreading pavements
Of men's careless works.
For the Earth must be made new!

There shall be a pause of thirteen heartbeats. Then shall the Priestess (or other so chosen) go to the north, pause to draw Power within her, and walk slowly once deosil (clockwise) about the circle with her hands directed outwards. All shall image in their minds that they are drawing in Power and sending it out through her as she says:

> *I call upon you, O Crone Goddess*
> *Of ageless wisdom.*
> *For our lovely world*
> *Has been despoiled.*
> *Whatever is needed, gentle*
>   *or harsh,*
> *Bend Your great powers*
> *To put it right.*
> *Blessed Be!*

All: BLESSED BE!

The Priest (or other so chosen) shall go to the West, pause to draw Power within him, and walk slowly once deosil about the circle with his hands directed outwards. All shall image in their minds that they are drawing in Power and sending it out through him as he says:

> *I call upon you, O Dark-Visaged God,*
> *Who governs the decline of the year,*
> *And of all things.*
> *You who are ill-favored by all, yet*
> *Whose great and cold Power is*
>   *necessary . . .*
> *Our most excellent Earth*
> *Has been despoiled.*
> *Whatever need be changed,*
>   *or ended,*
> *Use Your iron will*
> *To put it right.*
> *Blessed Be!*

All: **BLESSED BE!**

The Priestess (or other so chosen) shall go to the south, pause to draw Power within her, and walk slowly once deosil about the circle with her hands directed outwards. All shall image in their minds that they are drawing in Power and sending it out through her as she says:

> *I call upon you, O awesome*
>   *Goddess*
> *Of passion and of conflict,*

Who gives strength and inspiration
For the just battle
And to whom the hills and
    forests,
Streams and mountains
Respond as servants.
Our most beautiful Earth
Has been despoiled.
Whatever deeds be needed,
Call upon your followers
To put it right.
Blessed Be!
All: BLESSED BE!

As before, the Priest goes to the east and goes slowly about the circle:

I call, O golden God
Of sunlight and of joy,
Of all things that wax and grow,
Upon your joyous Power.
We need new forests, new places
Of clear air and pure water.
Grant these, O laughing one,
For a world which needs
Your echoing calls
And rough magic.
Blessed Be!
All: BLESSED BE!

The Priestess shall then take up the incense censer and first touch the ground with it, then reach as high as she may, saying:

I call upon you, O blessed
    Maiden Goddess
Of all things which are new
And rich with promise for the future,
You who bring beauty, and happiness,
And enchantment.
We need magic, love, and adventure,
Fertile lands and fertile waters.
Grant these, O smiling one,
For a world which needs your
    quickening touch,
And gentle music.
Blessed Be!
All: BLESSED BE!

At this time there should be a pause for a time of thirteen heartbeats. If it is desired, other workings may be done at this time, such as magic for the Earth, singing, and such.

The Priestess shall call for the attention of all, and say:

> *Let us stand now, and link arms*
> *For the Processional of Summoning.*
> *As we breathe in, and walk, and dance,*
> *May the deep Power of the Earth be*
>   *drawn*
> *Through our feet, and sent forth*
> *To protect and to nurture*
> *The natural places here about us.*

All do link arms and begin a procession which may become the "grapevine" or similar circle dance, accelerating faster and faster as all do chant:

> *WINDS FAIR, WARM LANDS,*
> *CLEAR WATERS, BROAD PLAINS*
> *SEND YOUR POWERS TO US HERE!*

When the procession and dance has reached its height and it is sensed that all have put much into it, the Priest shall call for all to stop, and drop to the earth, and remain in silence, saying:

> *Cease! Drop still, and silent*
> *Upon our Mother Earth,*
> *And let the Powers*
> *Cascade forth.*

All shall remain in silence for a goodly while, until the Priestess and Priest feel that the flow of Power has finished. Then shall the Priest say:

> *God of light and God of dark,*
> *We call for a balance in all things.*
> *May the excesses of the past be*
>   *banished,*
> *And a new world be born*
> *Wherein all living beings*
> *May have a place of honor.*
> *We thank you, O noble ones.*
> *Blessed Be!*
> *All:* BLESSED BE!

There shall be a pause of perhaps five heartbeats, and the Priestess shall say:

O Crone, Mother, and Maiden,
Eternal and all-encompassing
Threefold Goddess,
We call for cleansing of the
    Earth,
And a return of all which is
    natural,
Beautiful, fruitful, and good.
We thank you, O noble ones.
Blessed Be!

All: BLESSED BE!

The priest shall add incense to the censer, and offer it to all four quarters, then close by saying:

The Great Ones have been called
And shall remain about us
Both here and afar
Until the world be made better.
This rite is ended.
Merry meet and merry part.

Blessing
of a
Garden

 s the warm, sunny season approaches, our thoughts turn more and more to the activities we enjoy outdoors. Such activities are most meaningful for Pagans, for Wicca is by its very nature a religion of the open air, of forests and mountains, of clear, starry skies and firelight. The magic of the Craft will always work better in places such as these. But in the present world, these things are often unobtainable for the performance of our rites, and we must usually be content to work magic and commune with the Old Ways in a curtained room or within the cellar of a house.

Still, each group should try, whenever possible, to have rites in some wild and remote area; possibly this would only be once a year, but it would be rewarding.

Small circles, being often far less formal, may frequently be held by one or more individuals in a grove of trees, along a beach, or any place where there is some privacy.

There is so much in the way of magical training and psychic development which can be practiced while walking across fields or through wooded areas where the individual can be alone with his thoughts, yet so much closer to the spirits of Nature. It is strongly recommended that as much of this training as possible be accomplished in the open air for stronger magic and faster development.

When rites are regularly performed in a special outdoor place, especially one which is remote, it will "come alive" in both obvious and subtle ways. Growing things will prosper, and wild animals will find the area pleasing and appear in greater numbers. Pagans and even those who are even slightly sensitive psychically will soon observe that there is a definite "charge" or aura about the vicinity, and often wood-sprites and other elementals will be seen . . . first at night, and later even by day. This is the type of "enchanted woodland" mentioned in so many ancient legends of adventure.

This sort of sylvan enchantment can also become a reality in one's very own backyard through the regular performance of rites, and there are also charming practices found in the old folk knowledge which can help to bring this about.

When all is in readiness, the Priestess shall lead the celebrants before the garden shrine to light two or more votive candles.

THE BLESSING OF A GARDEN

It may be desired, upon moving into a new home, to dedicate the yards, trees, and flower beds to the Lady Earth Mother and to the old gods. If like-minded friends or Pagan guests may be invited, then so much the better. This rite can be performed as part of a housewarming.

In occupying any new residence, it is well to search out the most magical-feeling spot on the grounds. It is most appropriate to place a small shrine there to the ancient nature divinities, commonly done by erecting a small statue of the Lady. Although an Aphrodite statue is customary, it is quite acceptable to place a Madonna there . . . for after all, Mary is indeed an aspect of the Goddess! The statue may be set in the open or within an enclosure or grotto of your own construction, requiring only a flat altar-stone before Her image for offerings and an occasional candle.

Any weeding, cultivation, trimming or other care should be rendered a day or two in advance of the rite of blessing the garden, and the garden watered and allowed to rest. Food should be left out for the birds.

Before one's guests arrive, one can place candles (in glass jars, for safety and to protect them from the wind) about in the garden. If one has an image of the Lady or a special shrine, it would also be appropriate to place a candle there, and perhaps, additionally, a leaf or twig from each tree or bush in the garden.

Sweet honey-wine, milk, and ribbons of many colors should be on hand for the rite when guests arrive.

Each of the guests should, with their invitation, be instructed to bring something "for the garden." Plant seedlings, decorative planters, wind chimes, and even fertilizer, organic pest repellent, and a trowel or a rake . . . all of these things would be quite suitable.

Milk and sweet honey-wine are then mixed in a chalice. The officiating Priest or Priestess instructs all to hold their hands out towards and over the chalice in attitudes of blessing, as the Priest or Priestess says:

> *We call now for the blessings*
> *Of our Lady, our Lord,*
> *And the Old Ones,*
> *The powers of the elements,*
> *And the strength which we ourselves imbue,*
> *All to potently charge this*
> *Elixer of power.*

A portion of this mixture is then poured out upon

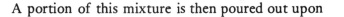

the ground before the shrine, with the blessing:

Gracious Goddess!
Powerful God!
O Guardians of the Quarters!
Powers of the Elements!
We seek your blessings upon this place.
May it be a place of happiness and love!
A place of refuge and peace,
A place of enchantment!
So may it be!

The priestess and priest then lead the group to a place which they have previously chosen, and there a new plant is placed in the earth and watered. A portion of the libation mixture is also poured out upon the ground.

After this, a number of bright colored ribbons are provided: then each guest present may take the ribbons and tie them around the trees growing in the garden, so that each tree gets one ribbon. As each tree is thus decorated, it is charged with the words:

I consecrate you, tree
As a guardian of this place.
I consecrate you before the Gods!

The priest pours a small libation before each tree. If she is a dancer, the priestess may call for music and dance thrice deosil about each tree in the style which she prefers. Afterwards, or instead, she should lead a procession or dance of all the guests about all the trees, in a deosil direction.

Then shall the priest or priestess call out:

We thank you, guardians of the winds,
The waves, the fires, and the lands.
O powers of the elements
Divine geniuses of Nature,
Be always present
In this place of beauty!
So may it be!

The basic rites thus being accomplished, it is appropriate to bring this ceremony to a close by consecrating the area with dancing, feasting, music, and other festivities.

Rites of
Passage

 n the first night after a baby is born, or the same night that birth takes place, the mother or the father (or midwife, if she is a close friend or relative) should take the infant out under the stars. The child should first be held up to the heavens, saying:

O Lady of the Starry Heavens, Wise All-Father,
Behold this lovely child _____ .
Conceived and brought forth
In love.

Bless and protect him/her
And grant the gifts of wisdom,
Inspiration, and wonder.

Dedication and Protection of an Infant

Place the child on the ground briefly, saying:

Hail Earth, Mother of All.
This is my infant, my love,
And my jewel.

Bless and protect him/her,
Granting your enduring and eternal
Strength, and steadfastness.
May he/she ever have a spirit
That seeks the stars,
And roots deep within
Thy loving breast.

One should then clasp the child close and look about for a few minutes, for those who are gifted with second sight are often able at this time to see prophesies for the child or the mother.

he rite should be performed as the Moon is waxing, and preferably near to an appropriate seasonal festival.

An altar may be set up if desired. Implements required for the ceremony are: the coven sword, or a wand if preferred, plus sword, helm and shield for the magical armoring. Candles may be used in the calling of the quarters.

As the rite is to begin, the priestess and the priest shall face the parents and the god-parents, and of course the child, who may be carried in someone's arms. The rest of the group shall be gathered about.

When all seems ready, the Maiden shall raise her arms in salute and call:

> *We do give greetings to one who is new*
> *   to this Mid-Earth.*
> *We present this small and sacred one*
> *   to the Old Gods,*
> *And welcome the small and holy one among us.*
> *Let us summon now the elements.*

The Sentinel of the East shall raise hands in salute to the quarter and call:

> *O winds of the East*
> *Who bring forth freshness, life, and joy . . .*
> *Cast your blessings upon this child*
> *And become a friend to him!*

The Sentinel of the South shall raise hands in salute to that quarter and call:

> *O warm sun and warm skies of the South,*
> *Bringing life anew, the growth of all things,*
> *   and promise of the future,*
> *Cast your blessings upon this child*
> *And become a friend to him!*

The Sentinel of the West shall call:

> *O cool lakes and deep seas of the West,*
> *Waters soft and giving of fresh life,*
> *Cast your blessings upon this child*
> *And become a friend to him!*

The Sentinel of the North shall call:

> *O mighty mountains and endless steppes*
> *   of the North,*
> *Meadows of green and the creatures that*

Rite of Paganing

therein dwell,
cast your blessings upon this child
And become a friend to him!

The Priest shall then invoke:

O ancient Lord of the Universe
We ask some portion of your presence here
among us now.
Shield and strengthen the child who shall
be dedicated in Your Honor!

The Priestess shall then invoke:

O most gracious and magnificent Lady,
We ask that some portion of your presence
be here among us now,
Give protection and shelter to the small
and sacred one
Who is here to be dedicated in Your honor!

The Maiden shall then sound the bell five times, and
then she shall ask:

Who is it that shall come before the Gods?
Who is it that speaks for this small one?

The Mother shall say:

Before our friends,
Before those of the mysteries,
Before those who are seen,
And those who are invisible,
Before the Lords of the Quarters,
And before the Mighty Dead,
Before the Immortal Gods themselves,
Do I bring forth _____,
We have long sought this small one,
And brought forth our child in love.

The father shall say:

Before our friends,
Before those of the mysteries,
Before those who are seen,
And those who are invisible,
Before the Lords of the Quarters,
And the Mighty Dead,
Do I bring forth _____,
We have long sought this small one,
And brought forth our child in love.

The mother and father both hold the infant, and the Priest comes forth and holds his hands out over the child in an attitude of blessing, saying:

> *May the blessings of the wise and joyous*
> *Father of the Gods,*
> *Far-seeing and far-knowing,*
> *Be upon thee, small friend!*

The Priestess comes forth and holds her hands over the child in an attitude of blessing, saying:

> *The blessings of the Triple Goddess,*
> *Of Maiden, of Mother, of Crone,*
> *And all of Their power be upon thee,*
> > *small friend!*

The bell is sounded three times, and there is a pause.

The Exhortation to the Parents
The godparents hand over the sword to the Priest. The Priest then holds out the sword, and the Priestess places her hand over his to symbolically hold it also. The Priest says to the parents:

> *I bid you both to put your hands*
> *On this blade of the magical Sword of the Art.*
> *And hearken to our words to you both,*
> *For the bringing of a new life into the world*
> *And the linking of one so young*
> *To the most ancient of Ways*
> *Is a most serious matter.*

Priestess:
> *I bid you both to give your child*
> *The finest and deepest of training,*
> *Yet make not his life one of tedious labor.*
> *For one so young must live well*
> *The joy of life.*

Priest:
> *I bid you both to give your child*
> *A home of love, warmth, and gentleness.*
> *If you have differences, moderate them,*
> *So that his world will know no disruption.*

Priestess:
> *I bid you both to respect your child*

As an individual, for he is unique.
Remember always that a small frame
*   and child's ways*
Often cover an excellent mind,
That in later years many shall honor.

Priest:
I bid you both to give always
A fair bearing to your child.
Have patience as he learns and asks.
And remember that you yourselves
*   once ran his path.*

Priestess:
I bid you both to give ever
New horizons, new challenges,
*   new worlds,*
So that your child may go so far
As his own mind and spirit shall lead.
Do you hearken unto these words?

Parents:
We do.

The Parents Vows

Priestess:
If you be ready to assume these duties
As parents of the small one
Consecrated before the Eternal Gods,
Then take these vows,
And say now after me:

(The parents repeat each line)

WE, _____, AS PARENTS
AND AS FOLLOWERS OF THE
*   OLD WAYS*
DO TAKE THIS SACRED VOW
BEFORE THE OLD GODS
TO WHOM WE GIVE HONOR
*   AND FEALTY.*

The Godparents' Vows

The Priest shall rap thrice loudly with the staff or wand and call:

You who would to this child be Godparents
Come forth now and stand before the altar.

The Priestess says unto them:

Are you now ready to assume the duties
As Godparents of the small one
To aid the parents in the upbringing
*   of the child,*
To support the young one that he may grow
Within the Old Religion and the Craft of
*   the Ancients.*
And, if the Fates and the Gods
Remove the mother and sire from this world,
To take this child into your own care
And see that he is brought up in the Old Ways.
Are you now ready to assume these
*   responsibilities?*

They answer affirmatively, and the Priestess and Priest take the sword to hold it before the candidates. Then the Priestess says:

Place your hands here
And swear before the Old Gods
That you are ready to bear these
*   responsibilities.*
If so, say now after me:

The Godparents place their hands upon the sword and say after the priestess:

WE ASSUME THESE CARES
IN THE ALL-POWERFUL NAME OF
*   THE LADY,*
AND OF HER CONSORT,
AND OF THE ANCIENT ONES.

The Blessings of the Far Traditions
The Priest shall rap thrice with staff or wand, and say:

I call on our friends of the Far Traditions,
Here with us as our honored guests
In this place sacred to the Gods,
To honor us with their blessings
Of this small and sacred one.

The Priestesses and Priests of the various groups come forward as previously agreed and give their blessings as they deem proper.

Closing

The child is held up over the altar and the final closing is given:

Priest:

> *O ancient and hearty one, Friend*
> > *and Helper,*
> *Crowned with the mighty horns of power,*
> *The far-traveller who sees all,*
> *Who gives wisdom and joy*
> *And the challenge of that which is new,*
> *Witness, we do ask, that* _____
> *Has by this rite been dedicated to Thee,*
> *And to the Craft.*

Priestess:

> *O gracious and most magnificent Lady,*
> *Whose slender hand turns the vast wheel*
> > *of the sky,*
> *Whose triple aspect does see*
> *The beginning, the life, and the end of*
> > *all things,*
> *Whose wells of mystery do give*
> *Inspiration and rebirth throughout eternity,*
> *Witness now, we do ask, that* _____
> *Has by this rite been dedicated to Thee,*
> *And to Thy Craft,*
> *O beautiful One!*
> *Blessed Be!*

A pause, the candles on the altar are put out, and the Priest says:

> *This rite is ended.*
> *Merry meet, and merry part!*
> *May the Gods preserve the Craft!*

HANDFASTING RITE

The bride, groom, and guests at this rite should be dressed in clothing of the medieval era, or in fantasy costume. Ceremonial swords may be worn.

This rite is best performed at the time of the New Moon. The place of the marriage rite should be decked with flowers of many kinds and fruits and vegetables in season. The altar should be arranged as usual, with a sword, a willow wand, and two white candles. Incense may be of a flower scent such as apple, rose, cherry blossom, or such. The couple to be wedded may dress as they desire, though it is an ancient Celtic custom that the bride wear a veil or net, and an article of red or scarlet. The couple should obtain and wrap a small symbolic gift each for the other; these gifts should be placed on the altar before the start of the ceremony, and are opened later on. Wine and a cake or cakes should be provided for the revel to follow. The Wedding rings should be given to the Priest just before the ritual. He will fit them over the wand and replace them on the altar. The groom shall wear a sword for this ceremony, and the bride should wear a jewel which she particularly treasures.

Somewhat earlier in the day, the Priestess or Priest should consecrate the area in which the rite is to be held. The bridesmaids shall pass the word to the bride that this has been accomplished.

To begin, the Priestess and Priest light the candles and incense. They turn toward the others in the rite, the Priestess to the right of the Priest. The Priest and Priestess join hands, raising their arms aloft at the same time, and the Priest calls:

> *May the place of this rite*
> *Be consecrated before the gods.*
> *For we gather here in a ritual of love*
> *With two who would be wedded.*
> *_____ and _____ come forward*
> *To stand here before us*
> *And before the gods of Nature.*

The two to be wedded come forward at this time, the man to the right of the woman, and stop before the Priestess and the Priest. The Priestess and Priest alternating, then invoke the spirits of the land:

> *Be with us here, O Powers of the air!*
> *With your clever fingers*
> *Tie closely the bonds between these two!*

Be with us here, O powers of fire!
Give their love and passion
Your all-consuming ardor!

Be with us here, O Powers of water!
Give them the deepest of love
And richness of body, of soul,
*   and of spirit!*

Be with us here, O Powers of earth!
Let your strength and constancy
Be theirs as long as they desire to
*   remain together!*

Gracious Goddess, Mighty God,
Give to these before us, we do ask,
Your love and protection!
Blessed Be!

All: BLESSED BE!

The Priest says to the groom:

If you do truly desire, O —————,
To marry this woman,
I bid you present to her
Your blade of power.
Pledge your weapon to her,
Unfailingly ever to be
At her service.

The groom draws his sword and, kneeling, offers it to the bride, saying:

Gracious and lovely one,
Accept my pledge of love to thee.
I pledge this sword, as I pledge my soul,
Ever to be in your service.
Like this blade shall my love be strong,
Like this steel shall my love
*   be enduring.*
Accept it, O beloved one,
For that which is mine
Shall also be yours.

The bride takes the sword silently in her hands and touches it to her forehead for the time of three heartbeats. Then she returns it to him and bids him to rise, saying:

My lord, I accept your pledge of love
As I do accept the pledge of your blade.
Thou knowest what is in my heart
As I know what is in thine.
The magic of my will, and of my love
Shall ever be yours.

The Priestess then says to the bride:

If thou dost truly desire, O ——————,
To marry this man,
I bid you present to him
A jewel of great value
As token of the love that you have for him.

The bride takes her jewel from her gown and, kneeling before the groom, holds it out to him, saying:

Thou who art handsome and strong,
Accept my jewel, my treasure,
As pledge that all which I am
And all which I possess
Shall be yours.
My love shall ever endure,
And shall flourish as the vine
And the tree.

The groom takes the jewel silently in his hands and touches it to his forehead for the time of three heartbeats. Then he returns it to her and bids her rise, saying:

My lady, I accept your pledge of love
As I do accept the pledge of your jewel.
Thou knowest what is in my heart
As I know what is in thine.
All which I have now, or shall have,
Shall ever be yours.

The Priestess then takes the wand and holds it over the top of the bride's head, saying:

Thou shalt be the star that rises from the sea
        The twilight sea.
Thou shalt bring a man dreams to rule his destiny.
Thou shalt bring the moon-tides to the
        soul of a man,
The tides that flow and ebb, and flow again,
The magic that moves in the moon and the sea;
These are thy secret, and they belong to thee.

Thou art the Eternal Woman, thou art she . . .
The tides of all men's souls belong unto thee.
Isis in heaven, on earth, Persephone,
Diana of the Moon and Hecate,
Veiled Isis, Aphrodite from the sea,
All these thou art, and they are seen in thee.

The Priest then takes the wand and holds it over the top of the groom's head, saying:

In thee may the Lord of the Forests return
*   to earth again;*
Hear the ancient call, and show thyself to men.
Shepherd of wild things, upon the wild hill's way,
Lead thy lost flock from darkness unto day.
Forgotten are the ways of sleep and of night;
Men seek for them whose eyes have lost the light.
Open the door, the door that hath no key . . .
The door of dreams whereby men come unto thee.
Shepherd of wild things, may you one
*   with him be!*

The Priest picks up the rings and wand and holds one end of it before him in his right hand, the Priestess likewise holds the other end with her left hand, the rings on the exposed wand before them. The Priest then says to the two before him:

Place your right hands
Over this wand . . .
And your rings . . .
His hand over hers.

The Priestess then says:

Above you are the stars
Below you are the stones.
As time passes, remember . . .
Like a star should your love be constant,
Like the earth should your love be firm.
Possess one another, yet be understanding.
Have patience each with the other,
For storms will come, but they will
*   go quickly.*
Be free in giving of affection and of warmth.
Have no fear, and let not the ways or words
Of the unenlightened give you unease.
For the Old Gods are with you,
Now and always!

After a pause of five heartbeats the Priest asks:

*Is it your wish, (bride's name), to become one
With this man?* (The answer is given by the bride.)

*Is it your wish, (groom's name), to become one
With this woman?* (The answer is given by the
groom.)

Does any say nay?

The exchange of rings then takes place. The groom
first takes the ring for the bride off the wand. She takes
the ring from him, placing it first on her thumb, then on
her index finger, then on the middle finger, and finally
on the ring finger, saying:

*In the name of the Triple Goddess
I pledge thee my troth
To love and cherish thee through all lifetimes,
For even though our paths may later diverge,
Yet will I always be thy true friend,
To love thee and lend thee aid and protection
By the power of the starry mill of heaven,
Beyond the imaginable reaches of time
        and knowledge!*

The bride then takes the ring for her groom off the
wand. He takes it from her hands as she offers it to him,
repeating the process, and also the same pledge.
    When this is complete, the Priestess then says:

*Then as the Goddess, the God and the Old Ones
Are witness to this rite
I now proclaim you man and wife!
Thus are thy hands fasted . . .
The Two are One,
The work of joy is done,
And yet begun!*

A kiss is appropriate at this time. The Priest calls
for the men of the group to step back and to raise a
sword arch through which the couple passes. Afterwards
may be held a circle dance of the guests about the
wedded couple, or a procession.

Rite of
Release

ne of the distressing things which are all too common to those of us who travel the highways is the sight here or there of some small creature which has been hit and killed by an automobile. Pagans, being closer to nature and feeling more kinship with animals, will especially feel pained at the sight of one of our "smaller brothers" who has been hopelessly mangled by the devices of Twentieth-Century technology.

To those who are gifted with some small bit of the Second Sight, it can be even more distressing . . . for the soul of the little creature is very often in the vicinity of its crushed body, bewildered and afraid, hence this rite is for those who would like to ease their way across.

When you have identified ahead of you the remains of a small animal on the road, take three deep breaths as you make the sign of the Pentagram with your right hand. (Starting at the top, down to the right, up left, across, down left, and up to the starting point). The hand should be making the sign of the Horns; that is, with the index and the small finger raised and the rest of the hand in a clenched position.

As you breathe in, feel and image as clearly as you can, that you are breathing in not merely through your lungs, but in through every pore of your body, breathing in the white, pure light which pervades the entire universe. Then breathe out carefully three breaths, pointing (if practical) with the thumb and forefinger of your right hand in the general direction of the small body, saying, either aloud or in your mind quite clearly in these or similar words:

> *Small friend, in the Name of*
> *the Gracious Lady*
> *I bid you to forget your broken shell*
> *It can serve you no longer.*
> *I bid you in the Name of the*
> *Patroness of things wild and free,*
> *To go beyond . . .*
> *To rest, to enjoy the Summerland.*

As you do so, picture again with the mind a glowing door off somewhat to the west of the body. A glowing portal which is open and through which can be seen a forest, or meadows, or whatever may be most enjoyable to the small creature.

Close with *"Blessed Be, small friend, and farewell."*
If you have some sensitivity in Second Sight you

should be able to actually see the astral body of the entity in advance of doing the spell. You may also wish to improvise some words of love and of comfort to add to the spell.

Rite For
the Dead

 f one of the grove or coven has lost a friend or relative, this Rite shall be conducted at the next sabbat or esbat near the end of the evenings ceremonies. Or a special, short ceremony may be held on the evening of the funeral.

If the Rite is to be held alone, the bereaved may wish to set out an altar and to read the ceremony quietly aloud, as if for the one who has departed. Usually, however, a Priestess and Priest will aid in performing this brief remembrance.

For the ceremony to be performed, of and by itself, a simple altar should be set, with four candles set about a central white one. A picture of the deceased and boughs of evergreen shall be on the altar. Wine and glasses nearby.

The Priestess or Priest shall, after a pause for silent meditation by all, light the four candles, saying:

> *O elements of earth, air, fire, and water,*
> *Grant release from pain, heal those*
> *Who remain here, in this more*
> *lonely world.*
> *And speed the soul of one who is loved*
> *Into the beautiful realms of the Gods.*

Then the central white candle shall be lit, saying:

> *Lovely, somber Lady of the Declining Moon,*
> *Strong and silent Lord of the Far Realms*
> *beyond,*
> *Be with us here at this time of loss.*

The Priestess and Priest shall stand at the west and east sides of the altar, respectively, facing south towards the one who is the nearest of kin or closest friend of the one who has died. If the kin or friend is a man he shall be called forth by the Priestess, if a woman she shall be called by the Priest:

> *O _____, we do call on thee,*
> *To stand here before us,*
> *And before the Gods.*
> *That we may give honor and love*
> *To one whom you have known*
> *Who has passed beyond.*

When the one is before the Priestess and Priest, with others of the group standing nearby, the Priestess shall say:

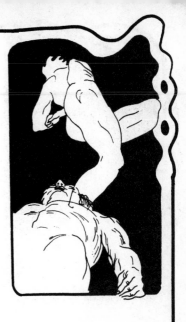

Good Friend, you have for a while
Lost one who is dear to you,
And we all feel your loss.
But it is only for a time,
And we bid you to have no sorrow . . .
There is a reason for being here
And a reason for going.
The Summerland, and the places
            beyond,
Are places warm, pleasing, and
            beautiful.
Will all ills gone, and youth anew.
So let us all be truly happy
For the one you love knows true
            joy at last!

Priest:

Dying is only a mode of forgetting.
A way of rest, a way of returning to
The eternal Source.
To be renewed and made strong.
To rest and finally to return.

Priestess:

We of the Old Ways know that when
            a person dies
The soul returns again to earth.
This has been a tenet of loving faith
Taught since long before history began.

Priest:

It is said in our lore:
"Arrayed in some new flesh disguise
Another mother gives birth.
With sturdier limbs and brighter brain
The old soul takes the road again."

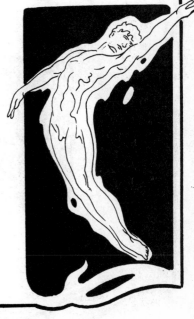

The Priest has wine poured for all present. All do face to the north. He calls:

O gracious Lady who gives rest,
O Lord of the twilight realms,
We do thank thee for guiding our friend
To the golden portals of the beauteous
Lands beyond . . .
Convey, we do ask, the love and good wishes
            of _____,
And for those good friends who yet remain behind.

The Priest turns to those in the circle and says:

I propose a toast . . .
to the Gracious and Lovely Lady.
Blessed Be!
All: BLESSED BE!

All in the Rite drink of the wine. The Priest then says:

I propose a toast . . .
To the strong, laughing, and hearty God.
Blessed Be!
All: BLESSED BE!

All do drink. The Priest then concludes:

And also do I propose a toast . . .
To _____, who now revels
In the glory and beauty
Of the Summerlands.
Blessed Be!
All: BLESSED BE!

Everyone drinks, then is the time to sit and relax, for the Rite is ended. All shall sing, joke, and generally make merry.

If it is practical, the candles should be allowed to burn until they go out.

ARCHETYPES: Extremely basic forms within the human psyche; the archaic "racial memories." Refer to the works of Dr. Carl Jung.

ASTRAL: A realm of existence parallel to physical reality but slightly apart from it. In this region both time and space may be traversed by the nonmaterial body. A wide variety of entities inhabit the astral: ghosts, elementals, phantasms, larvae, and the conscious or dreaming presences of living individuals.

ATHAME: The Witch's traditional magical tool, the consecrated, black-handled dagger.

BOOK OF SHADOWS: A compendium of Wicca rituals, spells, training techniques, procedures, guidelines, and other materials deemed important to a Witch or to a Full Coven. There is a wide variety of these Books extant, most of which have not been published, as they are usually considered secret. Each Wicca tradition is likely to have its own more or less standard Book of Shadows.

BRAZIER: A thurible or incense-burner. Usually ceramic or metal and often designed to be suspended or swing by a chain, and often quite ornate. Often partly filled with sand so that incense sticks may be inserted, or glowing charcoal briquettes placed inside to be sprinkled with incense.

CARDINAL POINTS: North, East, South, and West.

CHALICE: Ceremonial cup or goblet, usually placed on the altar. Considered often to be a magical tool representing Water.

CIRCLE DANCE: A ceremonial or recreational dance wherein the members of a coven or grove will link hands and move clockwise about a ceremonial area, facing towards the center. The basic "grapevine" circle step is "right foot cross over, left foot sidestep, right foot cross back, left foot sidestep," etc. It is free-form usually, with whirls, leaps, chanting, singing, and generally whatever the participants desire.

CONJURE: To work magic, usually by setting up an altar or central concentration point and focusing the mind by chants or invocations.

COVEN: An organized Witch group, with a Priestess and usually a Priest. Traditionally a coven consists of thirteen females and males, though usually it is less (about eight seems best) and almost never more. A nearly equal number of women and men is optimum, though it is acceptable with no male initiates available to have all women with only a male symbol or ikon on the altar. There are no all-male covens in Wicca.

CHTHONIC: Of or pertaining to the depths of the Earth. There seem to be rather powerful chthonic magical or psychic forces tied in with the structure of each planet.

CROSS-QUARTER DAYS: The traditional Pagan holidays which

Glossary

occur exactly between each Sabbat (q.v.) or Seasonal Festival (q.v.). These are: Lady Day or Candlemas (February 2), Beltane (May 1), Lammas (August 1) and Samhain or Halloween (October 31).

DEOSIL: clockwise or sunwise. The standard way of moving within a ritual area or consecrated circle.

DIANIC: After Diana, Virgin Goddess of the Hunt. A variety of the Old Religion which is usually all-female.

DISTAFF: Ancient spinning implement. In archaic times it was figuratively said that the Great Goddess spun the Earth and all things from Her distaff. In Nordic and Central European folklore, the line linking the axis of the Earth with the north star was called "The Distaff".

DUALISM: In theology, usually refers to the division of all things divine into two categories, Good and Evil. Judeo-Christianity is dualistic whereas ancient Paganism was usually monistic, with the belief that all things were a part of the divine.

ELDER ONES or ELDER RACES: In Pagan mythology worldwide, it is noted that there were advanced races, similar to our own, who either died out or migrated into other lands (dimensions?) either before the coming of humankind or early in our history. They were considered to have great magical powers and high spirituality. Also a few humans who have developed higher.

ELEMENTS: The magical and spiritual equivalents of Earth, Air, Fire, and Water, each having a wide variety of subtle meanings and implications.

ELEMENTALS: Magically or naturally created beings which have sentience and usually intelligence. These include gnomes (earth), sylphs (air), undines (water), salamanders (fire), plus a great number of nature elementals such as fairies, leprechauns, tree maidens, dragons, etc. Artificial elementals can be created magically.

EQUINOXES: The two times of the year when the days and nights are equal, Spring (March 21, approximately) and Autumn (September 21, approximately). These are two of the Pagan High Holidays (q.v.).

ESBATS: A Pagan or Wicca ceremonial time held between the high holidays (q.v.) and cross-quarter days (q.v.). Usually a full-moon rite.

FAMILIARS: Non-human helpers to the Witch. These may be animal pets who are trained to be "magical amplifiers" or artificial elementals created and maintained for magical purposes.

FEALTY: Dedication of service and friendship to another.

FESTIVALS: Times for Pagan and Witch celebrations: The High Holidays (q.v.) and the cross-quarter days (q.v.).

GOBLET: A cup or chalice.

GOD: The male aspect which pervades all of the universe in vast interrelationships of every possible sort, providing impetus, creative spark, and much, much more. It is capable of being perceived in many ways, depending often on the perceiver, and transcends time as well as space. Most perceptions of the various gods are valid in their own aspects and are or can be of considerable value. Modern Pagans will often choose the archetypal God of the Waxing Year as patron of all which is new and growing, and the God of the Waning Year as patron of all which ripens and declines, before the inevitable rebirth. Such perceptions enable us to form close emotional and magical links with godhood.

GODDESS: The female aspect which pervades all of the universe in vast interrelationships of every possible sort, providing emotion, creation, nurturing, passion, wisdom, and much, much more. It is capable of being perceived in many ways, depending often on the perceiver, and transcends time as well as space. Most perceptions of the various goddesses are valid in their own aspects and are or can be of considerable value. Modern Pagans will usually choose the archetypal Maiden Goddess as patroness of things fresh and new and growing, the Mother or Lady as patroness of challenge, passion, creation, and nuturing, and the Crone Goddess for patroness of wisdom and judgment. Such perceptions enable us to make close emotional and magical links with godhood.

GRIMOIRE: A book of spells, or sometimes also of magical training techniques.

GROVE: Nowadays usually used as the term for an organized Pagan group, similar to a Witch coven but composed of members who either are learning and training, or who enjoy Paganism for its celebrations and worship.

HANDFAST: A Pagan or Witch wedding. Usually it is for only so long as both partners agree to be together, though in some traditions it can be permanent.

HELM: Helmet.

HIGH HOLIDAYS: The seasonal dates of Spring (near March 21), Midsummer (near June 21), Autumn (near September 21), and Yule (near December 21 to 25).

IMAGES OR SYMBOLS OF THE GODDESS OR GOD: That which is chosen by a group or by an individual devotee to represent or symbolize an aspect of the divine by its appropriateness. Such objects must be exactly *right* in every way. One reveres the Goddess or the God which is symbolized thereby, rather than the statue, shell, tree, horns etc. which is the ikon . . . though in time these may take on considerable magical power by being so used.

INNER-PLANE TRAVEL: A technique of guided imagery wherein a symbolic, archetypal tale or legend is narrated and the listener follows along with her or his own thoughts and mental imagery. These are extremely valuable to the listener, since she or he can experience the story, myth, or legend within the subconscious, and absorb the very basic gestalt of it. Inner-plane journeys can also develop into astral traveling.

LUSTRAL BATH: A bath of symbolic purification, for the soul and spirit, which is taken prior to a ceremony. Usually a bit of salt is added to the water and it may be consecrated or blessed.

MONISM: In theology, usually refers to the acceptance of all the world and universe being one wholistic system. Ancient and modern Paganism are monistic.

MYSTERIES: The profound, metaphysical facts which underlie life, death, the nature of the world and the universe. Such Truths must be perceived not only with the intellect, but with the deepest part of the subconscious as well.

OLD RELIGION: Witchcraft and Paganism. So-called because they are, either by lineage or spiritually, a system of belief which existed long before the Judeo-Christian religions.

ONCE-BORN: One who has not been initiated into the Old Religion . . . initiation being a profound realization and understanding within the mind and soul, as well as a formal ceremony.

PATHWORKINGS: Any of the archetypal guided journeys undertaken in inner-plane travel (q.v.).

PAGANING: The presentation of an infant before the Gods by the parents, usually assisted by Priestess and Priest. This is customarily done between an infant's third and thirteenth month, though the custom varies.

PENTAGRAM: A traditional symbol of the five-pointed star, used as protection, or for invoking or banishing of magical forces and entities. Symbolic of humankind made perfect, with very many metaphysical meanings.

PENTON: A pendant or neckpiece worn during a Pagan or Witch ceremony for devotional and/or magical purposes. Usually it is some variant of the pentagram design.

QUARTERS: The North, East, South, or West parts of a magical circle or other ritual area.

REDE: Rule or law.

SABBAT: The High Holidays and Cross-Quarter Days are the traditional Pagan sabbats.

SACRAMENT: Food, drink, or love which is partaken in the honor of the deity and in either a formal or informal rite.

SHAPESHIFTING: The ability of a person to change into animal form or otherwise alter one's physical features, either physically or (more commonly) as seen by others. It is a magical technique of great antiquity.

SEASONAL FESTIVALS: The traditional holidays of Spring Equinox (near March 21), midsummer (near June 21), Autumn Equinox (near September 21), and Yule (near December 21 through 25).

SOLSTICES: The time of the year when the day is the longest, Summer (June 21, approximately), and the time of the year when the day is the shortest, Winter (December 21, approximately).

SPELL: A way of working some type of magic; to make things happen by paranormal means.

SPINNING: The archaic means by which raw fiber is spun into thread with a distaff or spindle. In archaic times it was figuratively believed that the Great Goddess spun all of existence from raw chaos into Reality. Spinning magic was used among the ancient Norse and ancient Germans as a solitary or group ritual. The Norns, the crone-goddesses of North and East Europe, were said to spin fates and destinies.

SUN WHEEL: The ancient eight-spoked wheel which symbolized the year, each spoke symbolizing one of the Seasonal or Cross-Quarter festivals. It also bespoke the cyclical nature of all things. The sun wheel is still used as a protective talisman. Its meanings metaphysically are very numerous.

SUNWISE: Clockwise or deosil (q.v.).

TALISMAN: An object with protective powers or the ability to affect chance or luck, usually worn as a pendant.

THURIBLE: An incense-burner or brazier (q.v.).

VITRIOL: The Medieval term for "sulphuric acid."

WAND: A rod or staff which is prepared so that it may be used for magical or psychic purposes, usually to project some form of Power. Traditional ceremonial magic ascribes to it the power of control over the magical element of Fire.

WHEEL: See "Sun Wheel"

WICCA: The Old Saxon word for "Witch" or "magic worker."

WICCANCRAEFT: Witchcraft or the Old Religion.

WIDDERSHINS: To move counterclockwise within a ceremonial circle or other ritual area. This is indicative of Chaos, and thus is considered to be bad policy.

WORSHIP: In Paganism and the Wicca, this means to "become as the Gods" during a group or personal rite, and to endeavor to draw the essence of a Goddess or God within, to see and to understand from their viewpoint.

ZILLS: Finger cymbals used in belly-dancing and in various types of dance magic.

Suggested Reading

It's hard to assemble a comprehensive listing of books on Paganism and Witchcraft. A few are good, many are bad, and a good number are a mixed collection of both. Thus a relatively small number are the ones we usually recommend to students who are serious in their interest. There are others, of course, and wide reading is always recommended.

Denning & Phillips: *The Magical Philosophy Series*. Five volumes on the Western Tradition. Highly recommended to the serious student.

Raymond Buckland: *Witchcraft from the Inside/Practical Candle-burning Rituals/Color Magick*.

Scott Cunningham: *Magical Herbalism/Earth Power*. An expert on nature magick. Very good reading.

Doreen Valiente: *ABCs of Witchcraft/Witchcraft Past and Present* ... and others. Anything by Valiente is recommended.

Gerald Gardner: *The Meaning of Witchcraft/Witchcraft Today*. Good material, even with a few flaws. These are the books that started off modern Wicca as a movement.

Anonymous (by Ed Fitch): *Rituals of the Pagan Way/A Book of Pagan Rituals*. Both are different titles for essentially the same body of rites. These are the core of the Pagan Way, and were designed and published as "public domain."

Robert Graves: *The White Goddess*. A superb work, even with flaws here and there. (His scholarship is sloppy sometimes and he tries to cover far too broad an area.) But an absolute must.

Robert Graves: *The Greek Myths, Vol I and II*. The most highly recommended work on myth for the student, it provides an important key for the understanding of myth and legend. Read it after *The White Goddess*.

Robert Graves: *Watch the North Wind Rise*. An engrossing work of fiction that summarizes much of *The White Goddess* and provides an intriguing "inside" view of a true Pagan society.

Wilhelm and Jakob Grimm: *Teutonic Mythology, Volumes I, II, III, IV*. Extremely long and difficult, but the best study extant on North and Central European pagan folklore.

Sir James Frazer: *The Golden Bough* (Unabridged) Another excellent sourcebook on legends and folklore.

Dr. Margaret Murray: *God of the Witches/The Witch-Cult in Western Europe*. Controversial but interesting historical studies.

Sibyl Leek: *Diary of a Witch*. Some bias by the author, but otherwise much good material.

146

The following do not deal directly with Paganism and the Craft, but are quite valuable:

Dion Fortune: *The Secrets of Dr. Tavener.* Anything by Dion Fortune is highly recommended.

Franz Bardon: *Initiation into Hermetics.* The very best book extant on magical/psychic training.

STAYING IN TOUCH

To obtain our full catalog, and to keep informed of the new titles as they become available, you may write for our bi-monthly newspaper/catalog. A sample copy is free, and it will continue coming to you at no cost as long as you are an active mail customer. Or you may keep it coming for a full year with a donation of just $2.00 ($5.00 for Canada & Mexico, $10.00 overseas, first class mail).

Stay in touch! Included are news and reviews of new books, announcements of meetings and seminars all over the country, articles helpful to our readers, news of our authors, advertising of products and services, etc.

LLEWELLYN'S NEW TIMES
LLEWELLYN PUBLICATIONS, P.O. BOX 64383-MR
St. Paul, MN 55164-0383, U.S.A.

FANTASY JOURNEYS
Narrated Quests of the Mind and Spirit by Ed Fitch

In this series of guided imagery sessions, Ed Fitch takes you on inner journeys to some very real realms of Magick where your Mind and Spirit explore and learn, create and enjoy, and come back enriched.

These tapes are based on Ed's extensive knowledge and years of practice and teaching. They combine aspects of Jungian Psychology, Qabalah and Magick, and the Pagan World Views into a composite of high technological application to fulfill your need for guidance into new worlds of consciousness.

TAPE 1

SIDE 1: THE ARMOR OF LIGHT. You will be led on an adventure during which you will find your personal suit of armor, constructed with your own hands out of resources from the inner world. Here is an adventure with real meaning in your explorations of other dimensions.

SIDE 2: AUDIENCE WITH THE SEA QUEEN. Moon Magick, Ocean Magick, the Lady of the Skies, the Lady of the Ocean Depths, Meet Her, explore Her Realm and gain the powers that contact with this Archetype alone can give.

TAPE II

SIDE 1: JOURNEY TO THE LAND OF YESOD. Within the Qabalah's Tree of Life there is a strange world ruled by the Moon. It is an Astral World with its own laws and strange powers you can learn to wield as you adventure through it with Ed's guidance.

SIDE 2: DRAGON RIDE. The Dragon is an age-old symbol of the active Female principle: creation embodied in a horrific and strange beast. On this quest, you will search out the dragon, understand it and harness its energies . . . or will it do the same to you, instead?

TAPE III

SIDE I: VISIT TO THE ELVISH HILLS. The true Lords of the Night are the Elves and Fairies. Meet them, understand them, and know their power. You will be rewarded, and you will never be quite the same again.

SIDE 2: THRONE OF THE GOLDEN AGES. The Tree is huge and powerful, old and venerable . . . its roots sunk deep into being. Climb the great Tree and discover the throne of a Demigod. Take its place, and know its power yourself.

TAPE IV

SIDE I: BUILDING AN ASTRAL TEMPLE. From materials of the astral world: astral wood, stone, air and fire, you build a temple of the soul. Your design, Your power, Your Symbols of Being are all incorporated into this mighty structure, built and filled with the power of your magick.

SIDE 2: VISIT TO THE CAVE OF APHRODITE. Journey to the beginning of Creation, walk with the spirits of Aphrodite's world of beauty and power. Here is the inner home of the True Pagan.

Each tape cassette is 60 minutes in length, priced at $9.95 or $32.00 for the set of four. To order direct, please add .75 handling per order, and .50 per tape for postage. For airmail postage outside. U.S.A. add $3.00 per tape, or $10.00 for the set of four. For Charge Orders call 1-800-THE MOON.